W9-AUW-622

Illustrated
# Jeep
BUYER'S GUIDE™

## The world's workhorse: Military to civilian

PETER C. SESSLER

Motorbooks International
Publishers & Wholesalers ®

First published in 1988 by Motorbooks International Publishers & Wholesalers Inc, P O Box 2, 729 Prospect Avenue, Osceola, WI 54020 USA

Printed and bound in the United States of America

The information in this book is true and complete to the best of our knowledge. All recommendations are made without any guarantee on the part of the author or publisher, who also disclaim any liability incurred in connection with the use of this data or specific details

**Library of Congress Cataloging-in-Publication Data**
Sessler, Peter C., 1950-
  Illustrated jeep buyer's guide

  1. Jeep automobile—Purchasing.  I. Title.
TL215.J44S47  1988      629.2'222      87-22064
ISBN 0-87938-277-5 (soft)

Motorbooks International books are also available at discounts in bulk quantity for industrial or sales-promotional use. For details write to Special Sales Manager at the Publisher's address

The name Jeep is a registered trademark of Jeep Corporation

Photos by the author, except as indicated

**On the cover:** A 1947 Willys CJ-2A photographed by Henry Rasmussen

Special thanks to the following Jeep enthusiasts for their generous help and assistance: Carl Walck, Andrew Magyar, Jay Sherman, Buz Bowling, Paul I. Politis, John A. Conde, Ed Hubert and Ed Conrads.

# Contents

# Introduction

What exactly *is* a Jeep? To some it's the small four-wheel-drive vehicle first seen in World War II. To others it's that snowcapped western mountain made accessible on a cold winter day. *Whatever* it is, the bottom line here is freedom. Jeep has always represented freedom because no terrain, adverse or otherwise, can stop it. With a Jeep you can leave the boundaries of civilization—really get away from it all.

The story begins in June 1940. With the inevitability of war just around the corner, the Army invited bids for a General Purpose Vehicle (GPV) that would most likely see use in Europe. There were several companies, among them American Bantam and Willys-Overland, which for some time had been hoping to land such a government contract. This was especially important for American Bantam, which by June 30 was broke. Frank Fenn, American Bantam's president, contacted Karl Probst, a consulting engineer who had previously worked on other projects for American Bantam, and asked him to design a GPV. Although Probst wasn't particularly eager to take this assignment, he was eventually convinced.

The Army specs were challenging. They called for a three-passenger vehicle with four-wheel drive, minimum 40 hp engine, capable of at least 50 mph, room for a .30 caliber machine-gun mount, a seventy-five-inch wheelbase, a thirty-six-inch overall height, a 1,200 lb weight limit, a folding windshield and a body made of easily tooled shallow sheet metal stampings. The weight requirement was later raised to 1,250 lb and height to forty inches. In addition, seventy prototypes had to be built within forty-nine days after award of contract.

Bids had to be submitted by July 22, 1940. Fenn had only contacted Probst on July 17, however, which meant that Probst had a scant five days to design the vehicle from the ground up. And that he did, with the exception that the weight limit could not be met. Yet as it turned out, the only other serious contender was Willys-Overland, which submitted a lower bid. It didn't matter though, because Willys could not deliver the prototypes within the required time limit and thus the contract was awarded to American Bantam.

The prototype was due for testing on September 23, and by working around the clock, it was actually ready by September 21. It had a wheelbase of seventy-nine inches, a three-speed manual gearbox, a two-speed transfer case, and was powered by a 112 ci Continental four-cylinder which put out 45 hp. The GPV was a success, even though it weighed 730 lb over specification. Bantam was awarded an additional order for 1,500 units.

By then, Ford and Willys-Overland had obtained copies of the blueprints (they were government property) and by November 13, Willys submitted its prototype, the Quad. On November 23, Ford submitted its prototype. All three prototypes looked pretty much the same.

Soon thereafter, Willys and Ford also received orders for 1,500 units each, the reason being the Army wanted alternate suppliers. The Willys Quad was the most powerful, with its 60 hp Go-Devil L-Head four-cylinder (both intake and exhaust valves were in the cylinder block), and thus gave the best performance. Ford's prototype, the Pygmy, was put together better, while the Bantam version got the best mileage and had the best brakes.

Unfortunately for Bantam, the Army chose the Willys version for the sake of standardization and designated Ford as the secondary supplier. Bantam did not have the necessary facilities to produce the GPV in the required numbers. The MA, as it was called, had a flat grille design, and the headlights were stilled mounted on the fenders.

The wartime Jeeps designated MB were slightly longer than the MA (two inches) and had the familiar Jeep grille. Willys built 359,489 units and Ford 227,896.

Willys took credit for the Jeep's design in its wartime ads. However, during 1943-45, the Federal Trade Commission held hearings in which it established that Willys did not *invent* the jeep. Much credit was given to American Bantam, but no credit was given to Karl Probst, who is known as "the father of the Jeep."

Willys copyrighted the name Jeep in 1946, and the source of the name is still controversial. Joseph Frazer, president of Willys-Overland from 1939-44, says he originated it by slurring the initials GP. In the comic strip *Popeye,* a character named Eugene the Jeep was introduced in 1936. In the army, the Jeep was known by many names, one of them being Peep, which later turned into Jeep after it was publicized by a Washington reporter who rode in one.

The Jeep was fantastically popular after the war, and Willys-Overland lost no time in introducing a civilian version, the CJ-2A. A station wagon, pickup truck and a phaeton (the Jeepster) were also introduced in the 1940s, all resembling the CJ. They enjoyed limited success, however; the CJ-series was in production until 1986.

By 1953, Willys-Overland had been absorbed by Kaiser-Frazer, but the company was still known as Willys Motors Incorporated. In 1963 the name was changed to Kaiser Jeep International Corporation and by 1970, Kaiser sold Jeep to American Motors Corporation. In fact, Kaiser had tried to sell Jeep to AMC back in 1961, but wanted to also include Kaiser's facilities in South America. It didn't cost AMC much to buy Jeep, $24 million in a stock and bond deal. And in 1987, AMC was bought out by Chrysler, for the Jeep product line. But whoever owned Jeep always used the Jeep name on its other vehicles.

Willys introduced the FC (Forward Control) trucks in 1957, the Wagoneer in 1963 (which is still with us) and the Gladiator pickups (now known as the J-series). The Jeepster Commando was introduced in 1967 and lasted until 1973. The most successful application of the Jeep name has been on the Cherokee, which first saw production in 1974. It was downsized in 1983.

You'll probably notice that Jeep products don't seem to change from year to year, as was the case with most American-made vehicles. Whoever owned Jeep never seemed to have the financial resources to make timely changes.

With Chrysler now in control, it is generally expected that Chrysler will introduce versions of popular Jeep models with Chrysler, Dodge or Plymouth badges. The first (as this is written) is the Dodge Trailduster, a Cherokee with Dodge identification. Interestingly, Chrysler may also introduce a version of the extremely popular Caravan mini-van in four-wheel-drive form with Jeep identification. From whatever angle you look at it, Jeep products are headed for change.

Jeeps are not sought after with the same gusto that other collectibles are. However, There are exceptions, such as the Jeepster made during 1948-50, but for the most part, Jeeps have been considered minor collectibles. I believe this will soon change.

In general, there are certain things to watch out for if you are looking for a particular Jeep. Originality is important and you'll find many Jeeps that have been modified, especially CJs with different suspensions and engines. These Jeeps may be interesting and unique, but from an investment point of view not a very good bet. If the Jeep you are interested in has a documented history, all the better. That in itself is worth paying more for.

However, finding a good Jeep is a lot more difficult than, let's say, finding a good Mustang. There are many more sources of good-quality Mustangs (magazines, clubs, shows and so on) than Jeeps. You may have to look further afield, but that too can be an advantage, because there are bargains to be found. There are a lot of Jeep owners who don't know they are sitting on a potentially valuable vehicle. And also remember one little known point: Automobile dealers, until the early 1950s, *could* and *did* send the titles of any unsold units back to the manufacturer so they could be "updated" to the current year. Thus you could have a 1950 Sedan Delivery with a 1951 title.

Jeeps are easier to restore than many other collectibles because they have body-on-frame construction. The suspension and drivetrain are bolted on a frame, and a body, in turn, is bolted to it. Unibody construction has been utilized only on the XJ-series (1984-up Cherokee) and can be much more difficult to restore if there has been structural damage or rust, because the body itself is a stressed member with the chassis components bolted directly on it. It will be quite some time before restorers start worrying about finding a straight 1984-up Cherokee, though.

Mechanically, Jeep drivetrains and chassis components have been very durable and rugged. Parts are available if you need them. The *real* problem with almost all Jeeps is rust. Many of these vehicles were used commercially and even with undercoating and rust-proofing, they all are prone to rust. No, they don't rust any faster than a Chevy or a Ford, but body parts may be hard to locate.

Another point to consider is horsepower. All the four-cylinder-equipped Jeeps are marginal in terms of acceleration if you intend to use one for everyday use. Whichever model you are interested in, try to get the largest optional engine available, which in most cases will be rarer, and thus more desirable anyway.

Also try to find a Jeep that requires the least amount of work. It may be tempting to buy a basket case, but it seems that almost everyone I have known who has done so has underestimated the final restoration expenses involved.

A final point concerns originality. What is "original"? Usually, any option that was factory installed is original, but many enthusiasts feel that dealer-installed options and parts can also be considered original, as well as the various commercial Jeep applications made by outside suppliers (such as ambulances, fire trucks and so forth).

*Whatever* "Jeep" means to you, I think you'll find that owning one will not only be a worthwhile endeavour, but fun as well. Few marques can claim the historical significance attributed to Jeep.

# Investment rating

★★★★★ The highest priced, the rarest and most sought after, these Jeeps are most likely to appreciate at a faster pace than all other Jeep vehicles.

★★★★ Still rare and desirable, the Jeeps in this category are solid investments and, fortunately, more numerous.

★★★ These Jeeps are just in the process of catching on and, accordingly, can still be very reasonably priced. This includes sleepers such as the Jeepster Commando.

★★ Still a Jeep, but built in great numbers, they are generally not sought after but may have good practical value.

★ This category includes any Jeep that doesn't have the original engine size and type; any customized Jeep; any race Jeep; or a total wreck.

# Chapter 1

# Military Jeeps

There were several wartime (1941-45) Jeeps that were used by the armed forces and the Allies. The bulk of these were built by Willys and Ford but, interestingly, the company that produced the first prototypes, Bantam, made only a handful.

Bantam, after successful tests of its prototype in September 1940, was awarded a contract for 1,500 units. This was designated the Bantam BRC 40 (1940 Bantam Reconnaissance Car). Most of these were shipped to Great Britain and Russia under the Lend-Lease Program. Later in 1941, Bantam was awarded a contract for an additional 1,175 units, and these too, ended up overseas. Today very few of the Bantam Jeeps have survived. Bantam was not awarded further contracts because it did not have the production facilities for mass production. Bantam did build torpedo motors, aircraft landing gear and amphibious ¼ ton Jeep trailers for the duration of the war.

Ford, too, was awarded a 1,500 unit contract based on its Pygmy prototype. These were known as the Ford GP (General Purpose). Like the Bantam BRC 40, most of these ended up overseas. Ford also built an additional 2,150 units under a new contract in 1941 and the bulk of these were shipped to the Soviet Union.

Willys also built, 1,500 units based on its Quad prototype. These were known as the MA. Unlike the Quad, these had a rectangular, flat grille, but the headlights were still mounted on top of the fenders. The MA also had very low body side cut-outs, not advantageous for amphibious use. These too, for the most part, were sent to Russia under the Lend-Lease Program.

The first large-scale production contract for 16,000 units was awarded to Willys because the Army felt that the Willys version best suited its need. It had the most powerful engine, and also Willys submitted the lowest bid. This version was known as the MB. It differed from the MA in many details, but the most obvious is that the Ford GP front end design was incorporated. It was heavier, weighing some 2,453 lb, a far cry from the original Bantam specs of 1,300 lb. The first 25,808 MBs used the Ford-type grille, but the rest used the grille that became the Jeep trademark.

Interestingly, after the MB became the official, standardized Jeep, Ford with its enormous production capacity was asked to produce the MB as well. This was known as the Ford GPW (General Purpose-Willys) and most parts do interchange. However, the Ford version was considered to be built better. Ford built 277,896 units and Willys 359,489. Although the MB itself did not change during the war, it was built in many, many variations: amphibious versions, ambulances, airborne versions, tractors, half-tracks and so on.

By 1949, the Army asked Willys to design a new Jeep vehicle to meet its current needs. Willys produced the MC, basically a militarized version of the then-current civilian

CJ-3A. They were very similar in size and dimensions and many body parts were interchangeable. However, the MC body and chassis parts were heavier, and the MC also used a 24-volt electrical system. In addition, the MC used a unique vent tube system which connected the engine, transmission, transfer case and gas tank to the air cleaner. These tubes were part of a system which allowed these components to be vented while the Jeep was driven completely submerged. Some 60,345 MCs were built between 1949 and 1952. The Army designation for the MC was M-38.

The Willys MD (Army designation M-38A1) was the militarized version of the CJ-5 introduced in 1954. Production of the M-38A1 continued until the late sixties. The CJ-6 military version was known as the M170 and the military version of the CJ-3B was known as the M606.

There have been very many variations of these, but it was the M151 Jeep that eventually replaced the Willys-designed military Jeeps. The first prototypes were built in 1959 and by 1960, the Army began to phase them in.

The M151 (originally known as the Mutt) was built by Ford to government specs and it was quite different from previous Jeeps. It featured four-wheel independent suspension via coil springs, more horsepower, a four-speed manual transmission with a single-speed transfer case and better ground clearance. The independent rear, however, caused handling problems (of the rollover variety) because it gave very little warning when it approached the rollover point. Because of

Willys Quad prototype. John A. Conde collection

Willys MA featured many refinements over the Quad. Note flat rectangular grille, redesigned side-body cut-outs, windshield design. John A. Conde collection

this and some lawsuits, the M151A2 with a solid rear axle replaced the independent-rear M151s. Although the M151 was built by Ford, Kaiser and AMC built these as well.

Because of the rollover problem, the M151 is not sold to the public when they become surplus. In the 1970s, any surplus M151 was cut in half before being sold to the public and, later, even quartered, but it was easy for the enthusiast to weld it back together. The government's current policy is to crush any M151s going out of service, but some do sneak by, which makes them an instant collectible.

Finally, there is the Mighty Mite (M422), built by American Motors 1960-63. This vehicle was manufactured for use by the Marines in particularly severe conditions (rice paddies, muddy deltas) and it was quite different from other military Jeeps.

It was powered by a 79 ci air-cooled V-4 Wisconsin engine. It had four-wheel independent suspension, inboard brakes, an aluminum body and a 65 in wheelbase (M422A1, 71 in. wheelbase). It weighed 1,740 lb and in an emergency it was designed to run on only three wheels because it was balanced so well. About 4,000 were built.

Today, the M151A2 is being phased out and replaced by a trucklike vehicle built by LTV. It features a fiberglass body, diesel engine and it is not based on previous Jeep designs.

If you are interested in a military Jeep, you should take note that many of the Willys-based Jeeps were built abroad under license. For example, Hotchkiss (a French company) has been making virtual copies of the MB for many years now. You may think you have located an original MB when it only may be an MB built by Hotchkiss in 1975!

Ford GP. Inset shows famous Bill Mauldin cartoon which captured the affection the GIs had for the wartime Jeep. Paul I. Politis

The first 25,808 Willys MBs had the Ford GP grille. Paul I. Politis

MBs on the production line. Paul I. Politis

MBs awaiting shipment in 1942. Buz Bowling

This is a partially restored MB. Unit originally
had Greek army markings.

Fully restored Ford GPW.

MB dash shows how little the CJ dash changed over the years. MBs had glovebox.

Four-cylinder Go-Devil engine. Not very powerful but extremely reliable.

Small rear seat is flanked by two storage bins.

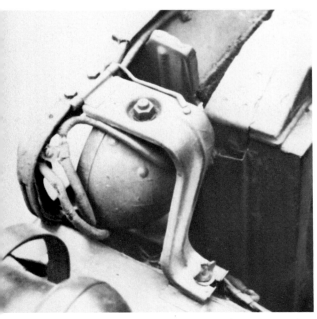

Underside view of MB. Buz Bowling

Headlight on the MB was designed to swing back to light up the engine compartment.

M-38 with hardtop. Buz Bowling

This interesting factory photo shows, from left to right, the Willis Quad, MB, M-38 and M38A1.
Buz Bowling

Restored M38A1. Buz Bowling

M-38A1 without cannon mounted. Buz Bowling

1952 Jeep trailer. Buz Bowling

M 38A1 with cannon. John A. Conde collection

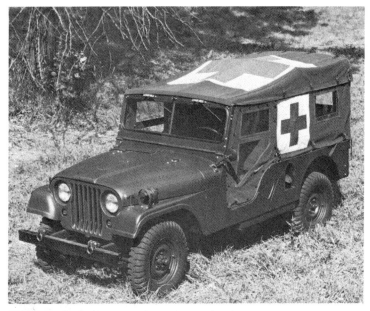

M170 ambulance was based on the long-wheelbase CJ-6. Buz Bowling

Rare and unique Mighty Mite. Buz Bowling

M151A1 has a horizontal-slotted grille. The M151 is the last true military Jeep. Buz Bowling

M151A2 has a slightly different front fender design. Note front suspension lower control arms. Buz Bowling

This 1961 Army photo shows how the M151 is stored. Note how rear wheels hang—typical of an independent rear suspension. Buz Bowling

# Chapter 2

# The CJs

| | |
|---|---|
| ★★★★★ | CJ-2A, 1945-49 |
| ★★★★★ | CJ-3A, 1946-53 |
| ★★★★ | CJ-3B, 1953-64 |
| ★★★ | CJ-5, 1955-83 |
| ★★★ | CJ-6, 1955-76 |
| ★★★ | CJ-7, 1976-86 |
| ★★★ | Scrambler (CJ-8) 1981-86 |

### CJ-2A

The CJ-2A was the first civilian Jeep that Willys introduced. It was very similar to the MB jeep produced during the war, but there were differences. They both used the same eighty-inch wheelbase, same 60 hp L-Head Go-Devil four-cylinder engine, same suspension (leaf springs at all four corners), brakes and transmission. However, the CJ-2A had a tailgate, side-mounted spare and larger headlights.

Willys heavily promoted the CJ for use in industry and on the farm. One of the advantages of the CJ was that it was available with front, center or rear power takeoffs. In spite of the fact that 214,202 CJ-2As were built, they are a good bet in terms of appreciation. Not many have survived in original condition, however. What you'll probably find are either restorations or modified versions.

A nice feature of the CJs is that they are very easy to work on. The engine and drivetrain are easily accessible, and with a few hand tools you can remove the body. The wartime jeeps were designed to be serviced and repaired quickly, especially under adverse conditions. And although, as the years passed, the CJs got a little more complex, they are still extremely easy to work on.

### CJ-3A

The next development of the CJ occurred in 1948 when the CJ-3A was introduced. Very similar to the CJ-2A in appearance, it featured a one-piece windshield and some mechanical improvements (stronger transfer case and transmission). Production continued until 1953, with 131,843 units built.

### CJ-3B

The CJ-3B was introduced in late 1952, and was the first Jeep to have a noticeable body-styling change. It incorporated a taller grille and hood to accommodate the new Hurricane F-Head four-cylinder engine. Although displacement was still the same, at 134 ci, with the L-Head Go-Devil, the Hurricane featured a revised valvetrain. The intake valve was located in the cylinder head, but the exhaust valve was still in the block. This proved to be more efficient and horsepower rating went up to seventy-five.

The power increase was certainly an improvement, but the CJ sure could have used more power. The CJ-3B remained in production until 1968. Production totaled 155,494.

Along with the CJ-3s, Willys offered a line of Dispatcher Jeeps, basically CJs but only in two-wheel-drive form. These were the DJ-3As which saw use as postal delivery vehicles and other specialized functions. Probably the most interesting of these are the Surrey Gala DJ-3A, which first saw use in an Acapulco resort. According to Andrew Magyar, perhaps at the most, 1,500-2,000 of these were built and today are one of the rarest CJ derivatives.

### CJ-5

The CJ-5, introduced in 1955, was essentially the civilian version of the M-38A1 military Jeep that Willys was producing for the

The first civilian Jeep, the CJ-2A. This pristine
restoration belongs to Carl Walck.

Windshield pivots. Passenger wiper must be manually operated.

military. It was referred to as the Universal Jeep, and this designation continued until AMC absorbed Kaiser Jeep in 1970. Its main styling change was the rounded front fenders, which continued on all subsequent Jeeps.

However, it was a slightly larger vehicle than the CJ-3B. Wheelbase was upped one inch to eighty-one, overall length increased to 135.5 inches (versus 129.75), and the CJ-5 was also slightly wider at 71.75 inches (versus 68.75). This translated into a cargo bed that was three inches longer, and a 100 lb increase in payload capacity. Wheelbase was again increased in 1972, to eighty-four inches, to accommodate the longer AMC-designed engines.

The standard engine, the Hurricane F-Head four-cylinder, continued until 1971. A welcome addition, though, was the Daunt-

CJ-2A interior is functional. Unlike the MB, the CJ-2A does not have a glovebox.

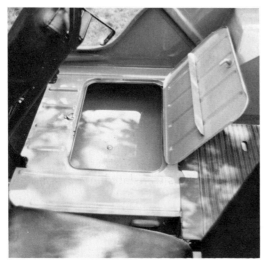

Storage compartment underneath passenger seat. This was standard equipment on all Jeeps until 1976 when it was no longer available.

Rear power takeoff was an available option. Note side-mounted spare. The CJ-2A used only one taillight, on the left. A reflector was used on the right side.

Go-Devil four-cylinder engine was standard equipment on the CJ-2A and CJ-3A.

less V-6 that was first made available as an option in 1965. This was the Buick 225 ci V-6 that Kaiser had purchased from General Motors. Although it was a great design, lack of popularity was the primary reason GM decided to sell the tooling and rights to Kaiser. The great horsepower power race was in full swing where cubic inches was king, and a small, yet efficient V-6 didn't quite fit into the scheme of things. However, as we all know, by 1975 the situation had drastically changed, and GM bought back the engine tooling and rights from AMC.

So, if you are looking for a pre-AMC CJ-5, the V-6-equipped version is the one to buy.

Beginning with the 1972 model year, AMC-designed engines were installed in the CJ-5, ranging from 100 to 150 hp. The base engine was the 232 ci inline six, with a 258 ci

This 1946 CJ-2A has an aftermarket Sears steel top. Small windows give the Jeep an almost sinister appearance.

version optional. However, for the first time a V-8 was available, measuring 304 ci and putting out 150 hp. Unfortunately, the V-8 was dropped after 1981.

For those interested in acceleration, the 304 is easy to modify. Also, larger-displacement AMC engines measuring 360, 390 or 401 ci are an easy swap because they *look* identical to the 304. The larger displacement is arrived at by altering bore and stroke. Naturally, such engine swaps are generally frowned upon from a collector point of view, but you will maintain more originality than by putting in another brand.

The year 1980 saw the introduction of yet another engine in the CJ-5. This was the 151 ci Iron Duke four-cylinder that AMC bought from Pontiac. Primarily brought about by the second energy crisis in 1979, this four-cylinder was the base engine until 1983. It wasn't a very popular unit though, and most dealers still ordered their CJs with the AMC inline six.

A significant improvement occurred in 1977, when for the first time manual front disc brakes (power optional) became available. Very worthwhile.

During the 1950s and 1960s, the CJs were still generally considered utility vehicles. However, by the 1970s, greater and greater emphasis was placed on the fact that Jeeps were "fun" vehicles, and Jeeps began to appeal to different people. Comfort options became popular, such as power steering and brakes, carpeting and air-conditioning. No longer was the CJ limited to use on the farm or at the local service station.

On December 21, 1980, CBS aired, on its *60 Minutes* program, a segment that showed how dangerous the CJ-5 could be—how easy it rolled over. Whether or not this was true, the report killed the CJ-5 in terms of sales, and 1983 was the last year it was available. A total of 603,303 units were produced.

In terms of desirability, a V-8-equipped CJ-5 is probably the way to go, followed by a pre-1971 V-6. Limited-production models, such as the 1965 Tuxedo Park, are also more desirable.

As with the CJ-3s, there was also a DJ-5A available for a variety of commercial and specialized uses.

## CJ-6

Along with the introduction of the CJ-5 in 1955, Willys introduced a long-wheelbase version of the CJ-5—the CJ-6. It had a 101 inch wheelbase (104 inches after 1972) which translated into a twenty-inch increase in cargo space. In all other respects, it was identical to the CJ-5.

This CJ-2A has a steel half-top giving it an odd appearance. Soft or hard half-tops have been

available from several aftermarket suppliers as well as the factory. P. Morrow

Not very popular, the CJ-6 did not sell well, yet it survived until 1976. An export model, the CJ-6A continued through 1981.

## CJ-7

The CJ-7 was introduced in 1976 and had some notable features. Its wheelbase was 93.4 inches, which put it in between the CJ-5 and CJ-6. More importantly, it was the first CJ to be offered with an automatic transmission as an option.

In addition, the CJ-7, from 1976-79, could be had with the Quadra-Trac full-time four-wheel-drive transfer case (with automatic transmission only). Coupled with an optional 304 V-8, a CJ-7 thus equipped is a formidable off-road performer.

Other than that, the CJ-7 was offered with the same engines and options as the CJ-5.

More and more emphasis was placed on luxury, and this culminated in the Laredo package. Chrome grille, bumpers, wheels, mirrors, fancy interiors and options such as air-conditioning, cruise control and stereo radios proved to be quite popular.

In spite of the longer wheelbase, the CJ-7, like all other CJs, is not happiest on the highway or driving around town. It has a jolty, bouncy ride, noise level is high, and it is a notorious water leaker. When it rains, water seems to come in from everywhere. The CJ-7 is happiest off-road. If it is not used

This CJ-2A has a soft top. William M. Cotton

Popular among military Jeep enthusiasts are trailers. They were exactly the same width as the Jeep pulling it. This particular example was made by Strick. P. Morrow

The CJ-3A has a one-piece windshield.

The 1946 Fire Jeep was built in limited numbers.
Andrew Magyar

These early Willys photos show the CJ-2A (also known as the Universal Jeep), a lot at the factory showing mostly Jeeps but a Jeep Truck can be seen in the foreground, an inspection line at the factory, and a Fire Jeep.

accordingly, then you miss the whole point of what a Jeep CJ *is*.

Many Jeep aficionados, rightly or wrongly, feel that the CJ-7 is the last "true" Jeep. Yet, whereas the CJs filled a certain need, the Wrangler in the same way is built to satisfy current market demands—off-road capability coupled with a modern, comfortable ride. A total of 379,299 CJ-7s were produced, so if you long for a CJ, they are readily available.

And in terms of price, they have not yet bottomed out because they are still considered just *used cars*.

## The Scrambler (CJ-8)

Introduced in 1981, the Scrambler was a pickup variation on the CJ-7. Mechanically, it was identical to the CJ-7 (wheelbase was 103.3 inches) and shared the same options. From a practical point of view, though, it was not competitive with the many small pickup trucks that have flooded the market. However, it is an interesting variant and should see gradual appreciation as it was built in small numbers.

Considering that the CJs were built in such great numbers, you'd expect to see

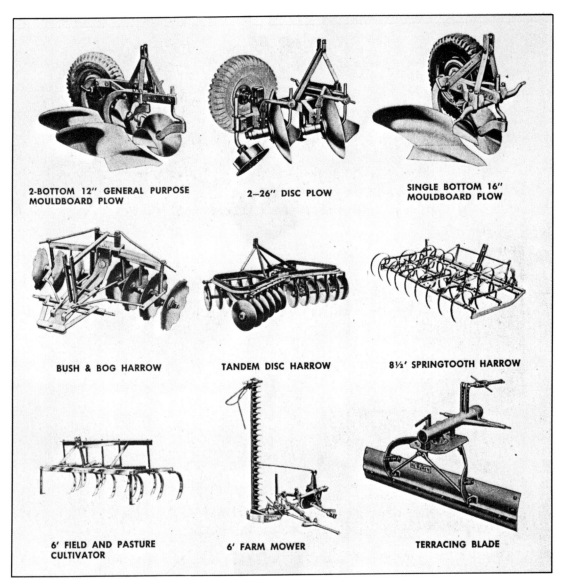

**2-BOTTOM 12" GENERAL PURPOSE MOULDBOARD PLOW**

**2—26" DISC PLOW**

**SINGLE BOTTOM 16" MOULDBOARD PLOW**

**BUSH & BOG HARROW**

**TANDEM DISC HARROW**

**8½' SPRINGTOOTH HARROW**

**6' FIELD AND PASTURE CULTIVATOR**

**6' FARM MOWER**

**TERRACING BLADE**

Willys made a great effort to show how useful the CJ could be with industry or on the farm. These tools were designed to be used with the Jeep. It was only until the 1970s that the Jeep started to lose some of its utilitarian image.

more of them around. This is not the case, especially with the CJ-2A, CJ-3A and 3B. The early CJs were primarily utility vehicles and were generally driven into the ground. The survivors are quickly being restored.

There are plenty of CJ-5s around, which accounts for their three-star rating. How-ever, a clean, original early CJ-5 is obviously worth more, especially with a documented history. Any original V-8-powered CJ-5 is also highly desirable, followed by the V-6s.

Although the CJ-7s are still considered to be just used cars, now is the time to snap up the Quadra-Trac V-8 version. Easy to drive off-road, it is also quite fast.

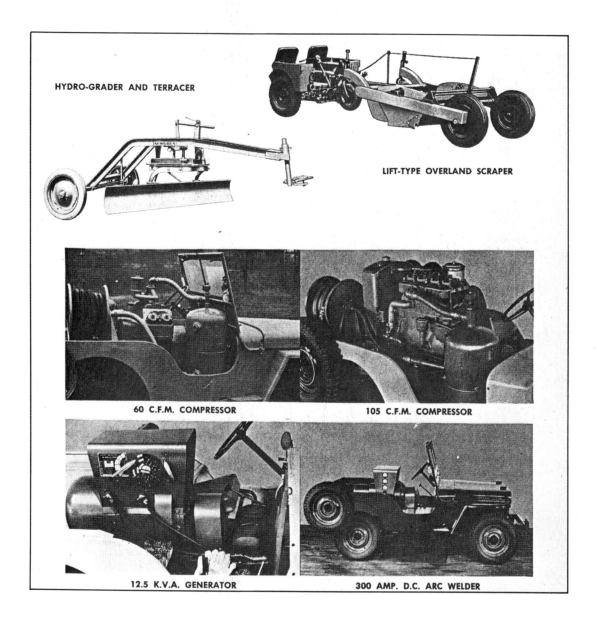

HYDRO-GRADER AND TERRACER

LIFT-TYPE OVERLAND SCRAPER

60 C.F.M. COMPRESSOR

105 C.F.M. COMPRESSOR

12.5 K.V.A. GENERATOR

300 AMP. D.C. ARC WELDER

This CJ-2A has a rare tiller attachment.

The FJ3-A Fleetvan first saw production in 1961. Built on the 81 inch wheelbase CJ-5 chassis, it came only in two-wheel-drive and was powered by the venerable Hurricane four-cylinder. The bulk of these were made for use by the Post Office, although a few were sold for commercial use. The Fleetvan did not prove to be a success, however, because of its small size and payload capacity.

## Jeep CJ Specifications

| | CJ-2A | CJ-3A | CJ-3B | CJ-5 | CJ-6 | CJ-7 | Scrambler |
|---|---|---|---|---|---|---|---|
| Wheelbase, in | 80 | 80 | 80 | 81* | 101** | 93.5 | 103.4 |
| Length, in | 123.12 | 123 | 129.88 | 135.56* | 155.56** | 147.9 | 177.2 |
| Height, in | 64 | 66.37 | 67.75 | 67 | 67 | 67.6 | 69.2 |
| Width, in | 57.12 | 57.12 | 68.88 | 68.6 | 68.6 | 65.3 | 65.3 |
| Curb weight, lb | 2240 | 2240 | 2243 | 2274 | 2413 | 2650 | 2759 |
| Clutch | Single dry-plate, all models | | | | | | |
| Transmission, std | 3-speed man, all models | | | | | | |
| Transfer case | 2-speed, all models except CJ-7 (Quadratrac opt 1976-79) | | | | | | |
| Front suspension | leaf springs, all models | | | | | | |
| Rear suspension | leaf springs, all models | | | | | | |
| Brakes, front/rear | drum/drum on CJ-2, CJ-3, CJ-3B, CJ-6 | | | | | | |
| | disc/drum on CJ-5, CJ-7 and Scrambler from 1977 opt | | | | | | |

*83.5 & 138.4 beginning 1972
**103.5 & 147.9 beginning 1972

The CJ-3B required a taller grille and hood in order to accommodate the taller Hurricane F-head four-cylinder. Windshield wipers were relocated at the base of the windshield.

This CJ-3B is equipped with a soft top.

Interior on the CJ-3B was unchanged. Large, thin steering wheel was finally replaced on all Jeep CJs in 1976 with a smaller unit.

This factory photo shows a CJ-3B with a Wor-man hardtop. John A. Conde collection

This is a 1954 DJ-3A. Similar to the four-wheel-drive Jeeps, the DJs had rear-wheel drive and a solid front axle. These have been very popular with government agencies, particularly for delivering mail.

The CJ-6 was never very popular in the United States, and most were exported. The extended wheelbase gave it an odd look.

This factory photo shows Edgar Kaiser (far right) with three other executives and the new CJ-5. Biggest visual change were the rounded front fenders. Styling on the CJ series remained unchanged until 1986. John A. Conde collection

Another view of an early, probably prototype, CJ-5. Willys on side cowl is unusual, as is split windshield and top-mounted wipers. Buz Bowling

1955 CJ-5. Note Jeep emblem on side. Buz Bowling

Factory photo showing a CJ-5 with a soft top. Side-mounted spare was relocated to the rear tailgate with the Renegade in 1972, and by 1977 on all CJs. John A. Conde collection

This is a 1970 CJ-5 with an original Kayline Luxair soft top.

1960 Surrey Gala built on a DJ-3A.

This 1971 CJ-5 is slightly modified. Engine is a
Dauntless V-6, the last year it was available.

This 1974 CJ-5 was originally powered by the 304 AMC V-8. Current engine residing in the engine compartment is a mildly modified AMC 390 which provides incredible acceleration.

The Tuxedo Park Mark IV was available in 1965. In some ways it was the forerunner of the Laredo Jeeps of the 1980s—offering chrome hood latches, hinges, bumpers, outside and inside rearview mirrors, and passenger safety rail. The Tuxedo Park also came with floor mats and wheelhouse cushions.

Bulge on bottom left of windshield houses the wiper motor. Beginning in 1976, the wiper motor was relocated behind the windshield.

Although it didn't become very popular, Kaiser did offer a camper option on the CJ-5. Paul I. Politis

Bench seats were not a popular option.

This 1972 CJ-5 has a hard top, winch and a push
bumper. Note side-marker lights. AMC

Rust is a major problem with CJs. You are better off to replace the entire body tub rather than trying to repair the rusted areas.

Removing the body shows the basic simplicity of the CJ—easy to work on and easy to restore.

1970 saw the introduction, on a limited basis, of the Renegade I. It featured a roll bar, rear swing-away spare tire carrier, gauges, padded dash, stripes and the Dauntless V-6. It did not have a tailgate and it was the first "sporty" CJ. Paul I. Politis

The Renegade was based on the limited production "462." Paul I. Politis

By 1974, the Renegade became a regular production option and it featured the 304 AMC V-8
as standard equipment. AMC

The Renegade has been a popular seller. This is
a 1979 CJ-7 with the Renegade package. AMC

1976 saw the introduction of the CJ-7. The longer wheelbase improved the ride and its introduction coincided with its entry (with factory backing) in rallies.

The emphasis on luxury is evident on the Golden Eagle available 1978-79, but even moreso with the Laredo introduced in 1980. It featured a fancier interior, chrome wheels, grille, bumpers and anything else that could be chromed! AMC

The last Laredo available was in 1986. This particular one has air-conditioning, tilt wheel and a high-powered stereo system.

With the gas crisis of 1979, AMC used the Pontiac Iron Duke four-cylinder as the base engine from 1980-83.

By 1984, the AMC four-cylinder was ready. It was basically the AMC six-cylinder engine with two cylinders chopped off.

The most luxurious Jeep made to date is the CJ-7 Limited made in 1982-83. It featured a leather interior. AMC

The last CJ variant was the Scrambler mini
pickup introduced in 1981. In 1985, the Laredo
package was made available.

Many enthusiasts consider the CJ-7 to be the last "true" Jeep. This particular example has been "Laredoized"—chrome bumpers, grille, latches.

# Chapter 3

# Station Wagon/ Sedan Delivery

| | |
|---|---|
| ★★★★ | Jeep Station Wagon, 1946-63 |
| ★★★★ | Jeep Sedan Delivery, 1947-62 |

Eager to capitalize on the success and acceptance of the wartime Jeep, at the end of the war Willys decided to build a passenger car that would retain the styling of the Jeep as much as possible. The wagon turned out to be extremely functional. Tall and angular, it was very roomy despite its short length and,

of course, the front grille was unmistakably Jeep.

And it was a wagon with a *difference*. It was the first all-steel-bodied station wagon; other wagons of that era used wooden bodies. At first, the wagon was offered in one color only, a burgundy (Luzon Red), but was

Initially, all Station Wagons were painted to simulate a wooden body, and most were painted Luzon Red.

The Willys-Overland factory in the late forties. Here, a station wagon body is lowered onto its chassis.

The Station Sedan received a different side treatment, an embellished grille and a cloth interior.

These photos show early Sedan Delivery prototypes. John A. Conde collection

painted to resemble mahogany and birch paneling. The Sedan or panel delivery version deleted the rear seats and blanked out the rear windows.

It took Chrysler until 1949 to introduce a steel-bodied wagon, the Plymouth Suburban, and Ford until 1951 to introduce its Ranch Wagon.

Initially, they were both offered only in two-wheel-drive form. The front suspension featured Willys' Planadyne ride, basically an independent front suspension utiliz-

1953 Station Wagon. The pointier grille and rounded front fenders were styling changes initiated in 1950 and remained until production end.

ing control arms and a single transverse leaf spring. Four-wheel drive was first offered in 1949 and remained optional until the end of production. As with other Jeep four-wheel-drive systems, the front end used a live axle with two leaf springs. Power was provided by the L-Head Go-Devil four-cylinder until 1950 when it was replaced by the F-Head Hurricane four-cylinder.

In 1948, the Lightning L-Head six-cylinder became optional until it too was replaced by the Super Hurricane L-head six-cylinder, in 1954. The final engine change occurred in mid-1962 when the Tornado ohc six-cylinder first saw service.

Styling changes basically paralleled those found on the Jeep Truck. The year 1950 saw the introduction of the new grille, rounded front fenders and the grille bar changes were the same. In 1960 there was a slight bodyside molding change.

Besides being a great investment, the Station Wagon and Sedan Delivery are eminently practical. Few cars today can match their volume and carrying capacity.

| Station Wagon/Sedan Delivery | |
|---|---|
| **BASE ENGINE** | |
| Type | L-Head 4-cyl |
| Bore x stroke, in | 3.125x4.375 |
| Displacement, cubic in | 134 |
| Compression ratio | 6.48:1 |
| Horsepower | 63@4000 |
| Torque | 105@2000 |
| Optional engines | L-Head 6 up to 1950, L-Head Super Hurricane from 1954; from 1950, F-Head 4-cyl replaces L-Head 4-cyl |
| **CHASSIS & DRIVETRAIN** | |
| Clutch | single dry-plate |
| Transmission | 3-speed manual |
| Transfer case | 2-speed |
| Front suspension | leaf springs |
| Rear suspension | leaf springs |
| Axle ratio | 5.38:1 (4-cyl) 4.88:1 (6-cyl) |
| Brakes, front/rear | drum/drum |
| **GENERAL** | |
| Wheelbase, in | 104 |
| Height, in | 73 |
| Width, in | 72 |
| Length, in | 176.25 |
| Weight, lb | 2,898 |

Rear seats are removable. Note wooden lined floor. Side-mounted spare was a standard feature on all Station Wagons with the exception of the Station Sedan where the spare was mounted on the floor behind the rear seats.

Interior, too, remained relatively unchanged.

This is a 1960 version. Side molding, one-piece windshield, two-tone paint treatment and different grille bar arrangement differentiate this version from earlier ones. Ted Dickson

In the interior, a different gauge arrangement, rearranged rear seats and no wooden floor inserts are the obvious differences. Ted Dickson

L-Head Super Hurricane six-cylinder engine.
Ted Dickson

1948 Sedan Delivery. Note pre-1950 flat grille. This one came originally with only one taillight, the other one is dealer installed. Also note single wiper. Jeff Lesher

Sedan Deliveries came only with a passenger seat. Unlike the Station Wagons, these came with vertical doors. Jeff Lesher

Pre-1950 Station Wagons, Sedan Deliveries and Jeep Trucks with the flat grille had either a 4 or a 6 on the grille to show which engine the vehicle was equipped with. Jeff Lesher

Lightning 6 L-Head engine. Jeff Lesher

This is a 1962 Station Wagon. Side moldings are similar to the Maverick version first sold in 1958. Jeep used to sponsor the television show *Maverick* at that time.

# Chapter 4

# Jeep Truck

★★★  Jeep Truck, 1947-63

Part of the effort to capitalize on the success of the wartime jeep was evident in the Jeep pickup truck first introduced in 1946. Its resemblance to the jeep is obvious and intentional. The Jeep pickup enjoyed a long production run with very few changes along the way.

Utilizing a 118 inch wheelbase, it was available in both two-wheel drive and four-wheel drive using the Go-Devil four-cylinder L-Head engine.

In 1950, the Hurricane four-cylinder F-head became the standard engine. The Super Hurricane six-cylinder became available in 1954. No automatic transmission was ever offered; a three-speed or four-speed manual was all that was available.

The only styling change occurred in 1950, when the front grille was redesigned. It became more pointed and used five horizontal bars. These were either painted to match the body color or painted white. The Station Wagon, which used the same nose more often than not, had chrome bars. In 1954-55 and 1957-63 three horizontal bars were used. The odd year was 1956, when only the top two bars and bottom bar were left in place. From 1958 to 1963, the pickup used a one-piece windshield, as did all Willys vehicles.

The Jeep Truck was offered in seven different variations to accommodate specific needs; however, the bulk produced were pickups.

Many of these pickups are still in use today because they are reliable, simple and inexpensive to maintain. Although trailing the Station Wagon, they are appreciating slowly and are considered a true Jeep collectible.

---

**Jeep Truck**
**BASE ENGINE**

| | |
|---|---|
| Type | 4 cyl L-Head |
| Bore x stroke, in | 3.125x4.375 |
| Displacement, cubic in | 134 |
| Compression ratio | 6.48:1 |
| Horsepower | 63@4000 |
| Torque | 105@2000 |
| Optional engines | 6-cyl L-Head from 1954; standard engine from 1950 is F-Head 4-cyl |

**CHASSIS & DRIVETRAIN**

| | |
|---|---|
| Clutch | single dry-plate |
| Transmission | 3-speed manual |
| Transfer case | 2-speed |
| Front suspension | leaf springs |
| Rear suspension | leaf springs |
| Axle ratio | 5.38:1 (4-cyl) 4.88:1 (6-cyl) |
| Brakes, front/rear | drum/drum |

**GENERAL**

| | |
|---|---|
| Wheelbase, in | 104 |
| Height, in | 73 |
| Width, in | 72 |
| Length, in | 175 |
| Weight, lb | 2,468 |

Early factory photos show a two-wheel-drive
stake body truck and a four-wheel-drive version.

Styling was identical to the Station Wagons.
This is a 1948 model.

Stylized initials were deleted after 1953 when
Willys was bought out by Kaiser.

This is a 1955 showing later grille style and fenders. Most Jeep Trucks had painted grille bars. Carl Walck

This 1955 has a rare rear power takeoff. Rob
Friesen

You'll still find original, unrestored Jeep Trucks.
This particular unit is only used for plowing.

Dash is identical to the Station Wagon, plain
and simple.

# Chapter 5

# Jeepster

The Jeepster is considered one of the most valuable postwar vehicles produced by Willys. Very reminiscent of the prewar phaetons, the Jeepster was available only as a convertible with sidecurtains.

Besides being a convertible, there was nothing new in the Jeepster. It used the same front-end styling as the wagon, same chassis and same driveline components, but it was only available in two-wheel-drive form. Two engines, the Go-Devil four-cylinder and the

Lightning six coupled to a three-speed manual with optional overdrive were available. However, the six-cylinder engine was only available on the 1949-50 models.

The 1950 version featured the revised front grille common to the wagon and pickup. It also received the Hurricane four-cylinder as the base engine.

The most desirable Jeepsters are the six-cylinder versions. In 1949 only 653 were built, and in 1950 only 1,778 models were

Factory photo taken outside the Willys factory showing a Station Wagon, Station Sedan, Panel Delivery, Jeep Truck and, of course, the Jeep-ster (at the top). Jeepster owners do not consider their cars to be Jeeps because they were never offered with four-wheel drive.

built out of a total production run of 19,130. The Jeepster is the only Jeep vehicle classified a Milestone car, and is an excellent investment.

**Jeepster**
**BASE ENGINE**
| | |
|---|---|
| Type | L-Head 4-cyl |
| Bore x stroke, in | 3.125x4.375 |
| Displacement, cubic in | 134 |
| Compression ratio | 6.48:1 |
| Horsepower | 63@4000 |
| Torque | 105@2000 |
| Optional engines | 6-cyl L-Head (Lightning) |

**CHASSIS & DRIVETRAIN**
| | |
|---|---|
| Clutch | single dry-plate |
| Transmission | 3-speed manual |
| Transfer case | none |
| Front suspension | single transverse leaf spring |
| Rear suspension | leaf springs |
| Axle ratio | 5.38:1 (4-cyl) |
| | 4.88:1 (6-cyl) |
| Brakes, front/rear | drum/drum |

**GENERAL**
| | |
|---|---|
| Wheelbase, in | 104 |
| Height, in | 62.87 |
| Width, in | 72 |
| Length, in | 177.5 |
| Weight, lb | 2,568 |

Factory photo showing 1948 Jeepster.

Factory photo showing a 1950 Jeepster with the redesigned grille and rounded front fenders. Note 6 on hood indicating this one has the six-cylinder engine. There is no question that the Jeepster was Willys' best-looking Jeep-based offering.

You can drive the Jeepster with the sidecurtains and top up, or with the sidecurtains down. Originally, Jeepsters came with canvas tops with red piping, not known for their durability. This is a 1950 model.

Jeepsters look their best with top down.

Grille close-up. Fog lamps are owner installed
and do have a factory look to them.

1950 Jeepster interior. Heater box was added by
the owner, as was a turn signal lever.

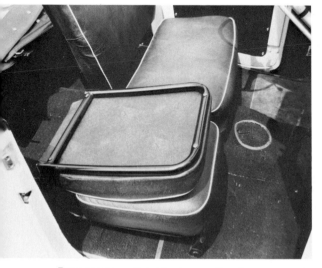

Passenger seat folds down allowing access to
the rear seat.

Engine compartment showing standard four-cylinder. Extra battery powers owner-installed air horns.

Close-up of the independent front end, which contributed the Jeepster's smoother ride.

This factory photo shows Doc Johnson's 1951 Jeepster, which has the distinction of being the first Jeepster to be reconditioned by Willys on September 19, 1959. It was one of the 300 1951 models to have larger mountain brakes. It is also the only one to be equipped with a factory rear stabilizer, clock, tachometer, front door armrests and an umbrella holder.

Rear-mounted spare gave the Jeepster a 1930s look.

These steps were designed to facilitate entry to
the rear seat with the top down.

# Chapter 6

# FC Trucks

| ★★★ FC-Series Trucks, 1957-64 |
| --- |

Among the most unique Jeep products made are the FC-Series Trucks, also known as the Forward Control Trucks. They certainly were different, because of the unusual forward cab location which was ahead of its time.

Two versions were made. The FC-150, the smaller of the two, was based on the CJ-5. It had the same eighty-one-inch wheelbase and drivetrain mechanicals. The only engine was the Hurricane four-cylinder, putting out 75 hp.

The FC-170 had a longer wheelbase, 103.5 inches, and utilized the High-Torque Hurricane six which put out 105 hp.

Common to both were drum brakes, front and rear leaf springs, a two-speed transfer case and a three-speed manual with a four-speed manual optional. The FC-170, though, could be had with dual rear wheels.

Because of the gearing (5.38:1 on the FC-150 and 4.88:1 on the FC-170) and modest engine output, top speed was limited to about 50 mph. They were trucks designed for local use only.

The Forward Control trucks were considered a marketing failure, however. They never really caught on, and they did have their share of mechanical problems (besides tipping over!). The front spring rear mounts were known to fail, and the front suspension and steering had problems too.

Like most commercial vehicles, finding one in good condition is not easy. Mechanical components are readily available; however, body parts are nonexistent. You may need to salvage parts from several vehicles to make one good restoration.

I feel the FC series has excellent potential. They are different, to be sure, and an interesting Jeep variant.

**FC Series**
**BASE ENGINE** FC-150 (F-170)
| | |
| --- | --- |
| Type | 4-cyl F-Head (6-cyl L-Head) |
| Bore x stroke, in | 3.125x4.375 (3.312x4.375) |
| Displacement, cubic in | 134 (226) |
| Compression ratio | 6.9:1, 7.4:1 high alt (6.86:1, 7.3:1 high alt) |
| Horsepower | 75@2000 (105@3600) |
| Torque | 114@2000 (190@1400) |
| Optional engines | none |

**CHASSIS & DRIVETRAIN**
| | |
| --- | --- |
| Clutch | single dry-plate |
| Transmission | 3-speed manual (4-speed optional) |
| Transfer case | 2-speed |
| Front suspension | leaf springs |
| Rear suspension | leaf springs |
| Axle ratio | 5.38:1 (4.88:1) |
| Brakes, front/rear | drum/drum |

**GENERAL**
| | |
| --- | --- |
| Wheelbase, in | 81 (103.5) |
| Height, in | 77⅜ (79⅜) |
| Width, in | 71⅜ (76½) |
| Length, in | 147½ (180½) |

FC-150 and FC-170 are probably the oddest vehicles to bear the Jeep name. They have a Fisher-Price feel and look to them.

This is a restored 1963 FC-150 pickup still used
commercially. Note spare tire location.

Although the pickup box was slightly over six
feet long, its configuration was a limiting factor.

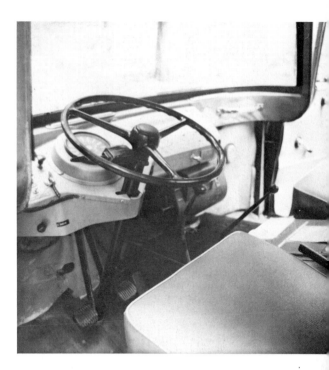

This is a 1964 FC-170 Fire Jeep. Note dual rear wheels.

FC-170s awaiting restoration.

Although most FC-Series Trucks came with a rear side window, a few did not.

Short wheelbase is evident on this unrestored
FC-150.

# Chapter 7

# Jeepster
# Commando

'Jeepster' Commando Convertible

'Jeepster' Commando Convertible

'Jeepster' Commando Roadster

'Jeepster' Commando Station Wagon

'Jeepster' Commando Pick-Up

The resurrected Jeepster came in a variety of configurations: convertible, roadster, pickup and station wagon. Paul I. Politis

The Jeepster Commando series, according to Kaiser, was designed to compete in the Sports-Utility market. It is one of the more interesting Jeep variants, and was deliberately designed to resemble the CJ, especially from the front.

It was offered in several configurations: a roadster, a station wagon, a convertible and a pickup. The wagon carries more than a passing resemblance to the Wagoneer. By 1972, AMC, which by then had exerted more control over the Jeep line, dropped "Jeepster" from the name and redesigned the front grille. Most Jeep enthusiasts feel that the new grille was rather ugly, and it no doubt contributed to declining sales. The line was discontinued after 1973.

The Jeepster was based on the CJ-6, as they shared the same 101 inch wheelbase (104 inches in 1972-73 to accommodate the longer AMC engines). The standard engine was the Hurricane F-Head four-cylinder which pumped out 75 hp. (If you are interested in a Jeepster Commando, avoid one quipped with the Hurricane. It just doesn't have enough power.) Optional, and recommended, is the Dauntless 225 ci V-6 (ex-Buick) which put out 160 hp. In 1972, the

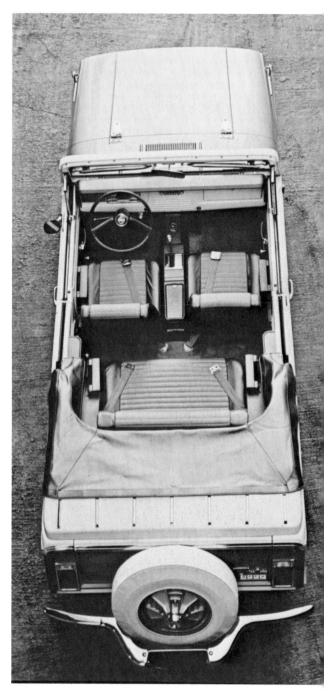

Bird's-eye view of the convertible.

**Jeepster Commando**
**BASE ENGINE**
| | |
|---|---|
| Type | 4-cyl F-Head (1972-73 inline 6 ohv) |
| Bore x stroke, in | 3.125x4.375 (3.75x3.50) |
| Displacement, cubic in | 134 (232) |
| Compression ratio | 6.7:1 (8.0:1) |
| Horsepower | 75@4000 (100@3600) |
| Torque | 114@2000 (185@1800) |
| Optional engines | 225 ci V-6 (1972-73 258 ci I-6, 304 V-8) |

**CHASSIS & DRIVETRAIN**
| | |
|---|---|
| Clutch | single dry-plate |
| Transmission | 3-speed manual (4-speed manual, 3-speed automatic opt) |
| Transfer case | 2-speed |
| Front suspension | leaf springs |
| Rear suspension | leaf springs |
| Axle ratio | various |
| Brakes, front/rear | drum/drum |

**GENERAL**
| | |
|---|---|
| Wheelbase, in | 101 (1972-73, 104) |
| Height, in | 62.4-65 |
| Width, in | 65.2 |
| Length, in | 168.4 |
| Weight, lb | 2,800 |

AMC engines were replaced by the four-cylinder and V-6. The base engine was the 232 ci inline six, while the 258 ci inline six and 304 ci V-8 were optional.

Transmission choice paralleled the CJs too. A three-speed manual was standard; a four-speed and a three-speed automatic were optional. The transfer case was the usual two-speed part-time unit.

Because the Jeepster Commando is relatively unknown, *now* is the time to get one. It has good collector potential—especially the convertible, which strongly resembles the original Jeepster made in 1948-50. As with other Jeep vehicles, rust is the major problem, particularly with an unrestored example. The 1972-73 versions, which were better mechanically, are not as desirable because of their odd styling. However, whichever version you choose, you can expect it to appreciate in value because the production run did not stretch into decades as with other Jeeps. They are relatively rare and unique.

Early Jeepster Commando prototype with a dummy top. Paul I. Politis

Rear view of the pickup. Box was 63.8 inches long but distance between wheelhouses, 36 inches, limited the pickup's usefulness.

In this factory photo, the pickup version is promoted for gas station use. Paul I. Politis

The AMC-redesigned Commandos of 1972-73 were offered in three configurations, station wagon, pickup and roadster. Convertibles were not available. Although they featured many engineering refinements and AMC engines, they did not sell well because of the styling.

Typical of the no-frills Jeepster interior, the
dash provided minimal instrumentation.

# Chapter 8

# Gladiator and J-Series Pickups

| | |
|---|---|
| ★★ | **Gladiator, 1962-69** |
| | **J-Series, 1970-87** |

The new line of Jeep pickups was introduced in 1962 to replace the previous Willys pickups that had remained relatively unchanged since 1947. The Gladiator pickup was based on the new Wagoneer, and they shared the same mechanical components, engines and drivetrains (see Chapter 9). Both looked very similar from the front, but the large, square grille that was changed on the Wagoneer in 1965 remained on the Gladiator until

Gladiator pickups have remained virtually unchanged (visually) since their introduction in 1963. Large square grille adorned the truck until 1969. Paul I. Politis

1970, when it was changed to a low, wide grille that extended the full width of the front of the vehicle.

Many wheelbases have been available, ranging from 118 to 132 inches, as well as short-box and long-box versions. Other variations include Thriftside, chassis cabs, wreckers, dumpers and so on. For the 1987 version, only a 130 inch wheelbase long box is available.

Following 1978, sales have been declining to the point where Chrysler finally discontinued producing the J-10/20 upon taking Jeep over in 1987. Sales have been dismal because the market perceives the Jeep pickup as a dated design.

Don't look for the Gladiator J-Series to appreciate in the foreseeable future either. However, it is a good truck from a practical standpoint, and can give good service for many years.

| Gladiator/J-Series | |
|---|---|
| **BASE ENGINE** | |
| Type | inline 6-cyl ohv |
| Bore x stroke, in | 3.750x3.895 |
| Displacement, cubic in | 258 |
| Compression ratio | 9.2:1 |
| Horsepower | 114@3600 |
| Torque | 196@2000 |
| Optional engines | 360 ci V-8 |
| **CHASSIS & DRIVETRAIN** | |
| Clutch | single dry-plate |
| Transmission | 4-speed manual (3-speed auto opt) |
| Transfer case | 2-speed |
| Front suspension | leaf springs |
| Rear suspension | leaf springs |
| Axle ratio | 2.73:1 (3.31 with auto trans) |
| Brakes, front/rear | disc/drum |
| **GENERAL** | |
| Wheelbase, in | 130.7 |
| Height, in | 69 |
| Width, in | 78.9 |
| Length, in | 206 |
| Weight, lb | 4,200 |
| *Note: These specifications are for a 1987 J-10* | |

Gladiator camper option. Paul I. Politis

PLATFORM STAKE

Over the years, the Gladiator/J-Series has been available in a number of configurations.

Like the Wagoneer and Cherokee, the interiors have changed with the times. Here is the 1972 dash.

The dashboard, vintage 1980, showing the smoothness of line and features, which are easy to read.

Beginning with 1970, grille design was changed
to resemble current Wagoneer design. This is a
1972 J-4000. AMC

1977 J-10 with the Honcho package definitely
gives the truck a sporty flavor. AMC

Honcho stripes changed every year. This is a
1980 model.

1981 J-10 in the rarely seen Thriftside form.
AMC

Unique roof treatment was discontinued after
the 1980 model year.

1987 was the last year for the J-Series. Zero
advertising and lack of factory incentives helped
to reduce sales to a trickle, especially after the
successful introduction of the mid-size Comanche pickups.

# Chapter 9

# Wagoneer

| ★★ | Wagoneer |
|----|----------|

The Wagoneer was introduced in 1962 as a replacement for the aging Willys wagon. At the time it was considered a fresh, modern design and it has always been Jeep's showcase vehicle. It has been the biggest, most expensive and most carlike of any vehicle Jeep has ever built.

It looks similar to conventional station wagons, and while it sits higher off the ground, it has always been a vehicle that your mainstream automobile buyer would not feel self-conscious driving. It combines passenger-car comforts with off-road capabilities. Of all the large four-wheel-drive vehicles that have been available during the past twenty-five years, the Wagoneer has had the most comfortable ride, without the hard-riding and incessant jogging that is typical of other four-wheel-drive vehicles.

The most obvious fact about the Wagoneer is that it has kept the same body for twenty-five years. The grilles have been changed from time to time, and mechanically it has been constantly improved, but

1963 Wagoneer showing original grille design. Although there have been a host of engineering, styling and interior refinements, basic vehicle has remained unchanged.

the Grand Wagoneer currently available is basically the same Wagoneer that was available in 1962. Because the body has not been changed, it has been a very good money-maker for AMC. According to some estimates, it costs a little over $9,000 to build a current Grand Wagoneer that lists for about $25,000!

The 1962 Wagoneer was available in six different versions: two- and four-door two-wheel-drive and four-wheel-drive wagons, and two-wheel-drive and four-wheel-drive panel deliveries (which used vertical doors rather than a tailgate). The standard engine was a Tornado 230 ci six which featured an overhead cam. Although it was a sound design, it did suffer from oiling problems. Optional in 1965 was a Vigilante 327 ci V-8. (This was not the well-known Chevy V-8 but one produced by Kaiser Jeep.) Standard transmission was a column-mounted three-speed manual, or optional, the GM three-speed Turbo Hydra-matic. A four-speed manual was added in 1965 and continued optional until 1972.

In 1965, the AMC 232 Hi Torque-6 replaced the 230. The 327 continued through 1967, but was replaced by the Dauntless 350 ci V-8 made by Buick in 1968. However, the 327 continued to be available in 1968 in the Super Wagoneer only. The Buick lasted until the 1971 model year, at which time it was replaced with the familiar AMC 304 and 360 V-8s. The big AMC 401 V-8 was optional during 1974-78. The 360 has been the optional engine in the Wagoneer since 1979.

AMC's 258 ci six became the standard Wagoneer engine beginning in 1972. None of the six-cylinder engines are recommended

1963-64 Wagoneers came with a torsion bar front suspension which was subsequently dropped because of reliability problems.

Super Wagoneer, first available in 1965, had grille change.

because they just don't put out enough power.

The Quadra-Trac automatic full-time four-wheel-drive system first saw use in 1973 and was a major advance. (The most important *disadvantage* of a part-time system is that if it is used on dry pavement, excessive wear and failure can result.) Quadra-Trac is a full-time system giving superior traction on all road surfaces and conditions. It became standard equipment on Wagoneer in 1974 and continued until 1979. In 1980 the Selec-Trac system became standard equipment. It too is a full-time system. However, through a dash-mounted switch, the system can be switched to either two-wheel drive or full-time four-wheel drive. The advantage here is improved mileage in the two-wheel-drive mode.

The two-door panel delivery, a model you don't see frequently, was discontinued in 1967. The Super Wagoneer available during 1965-68 was the predecessor of today's Grand Wagoneer, on which practically everything was standard equipment. The Super Wagoneer was available only with the 327 V-8, automatic transmission, power steering and power brakes, air conditioning, tilt wheel, deluxe interior and vinyl roof.

The Wagoneer is now considered a relic—it should have been updated years ago. Jeep's new owner, Chrysler, will most likely continue production and it is possible that eventually, we may see a redesigned Wagoneer.

| Wagoneer | |
|---|---|
| **BASE ENGINE** | |
| Type | ohv V-8 |
| Bore x stroke, in | 4.079x3.440 |
| Displacement, cubic in | 360 |
| Compression ratio | 8.5:1 |
| Horsepower | 114@3200 |
| Torque | 280@1500 |
| Optional engines | none |
| **CHASSIS & DRIVETRAIN** | |
| Clutch | none |
| Transmission | 3-speed automatic |
| Transfer case | 2-speed |
| Front suspension | leaf springs |
| Rear suspension | leaf springs |
| Axle ratio | 2.73:1 |
| Brakes, front/rear | disc/drum |
| **GENERAL** | |
| Wheelbase, in | 108.7 |
| Height, in | 66.4 |
| Width, in | 74.8 |
| Length, in | 186.4 |
| Curb Weight, lb | 4,750 |

*Note: These specifications are for a 1987 Grand Wagoneer*

1968 Wagoneer. Paul I. Politis

The 1973 Wagoneer was the first to receive the
Quadra-Trac full-time four-wheel-drive system.
AMC

Proving that the original design had a simplicity
of function that sold well, the Wagoneer changed
slowly through the 1970s. Here is a 1977 model.

The 1979 Jeep Wagoneer Limited boasted few
enhancements to the original design.

A 1980 Jeep Wagoneer Limited and approving
model.

The 1984 Wagoneer Grand carried subtle new
refinements to the lines of the original Wagoneer design.

1987 Grand Wagoneer.

Large load space is evident with tailgate down.
Rear passenger seat also folds down.

1987 interior emphasizes luxury.

Base six-cylinder engine is simply not enough motivation for a vehicle as heavy as the Wago- neer. Over the years several V-8s have been available and they are a necessity.

# Chapter 10

# Cherokee

| ★★★  Cherokee, 1974-83 |
| --- |

The introduction of the Cherokee came in 1974. It was available in two models, a standard version and the more luxurious Cherokee S. Built on the same 109 inch wheelbase as the Wagoneer, the Cherokee was actually a two-door Wagoneer. Mechanically they were identical, as were their interiors—except for minor trim items. In 1978 a four-door Cherokee was also offered.

Although the Wagoneer and Cherokee are almost identical, the two doors give the Cherokee a far more aggressive look. The 1978 and later Chief models—with a two-tone paint treatment, large wheels and tires—enhanced the tough-guy, off-road image.

Three engines were available on the Cherokee 1974-78: the AMC 258 ci six, a 360 V-8

1974 brought us the Cherokee—basically a two-door Wagoneer. AMC

Restyling the rear side windows gave the Cherokee a more sporty feel.

1977 saw the introduction of the four-door Cherokee. AMC

in two- and four-barrel versions and a 401 four-barrel V-8. The six is really marginal for a vehicle the size and weight of the Cherokee; one of the V-8s is recommended. From 1979 on, the only V-8 available was the 360.

Four-wheel drive was standard equipment on all Cherokees. A part-time system with manual front hubs was available, with a floor-mounted four-speed or a column-mounted three-speed automatic. Until 1979, the Quadra-Trac automatic four-wheel-drive system was optional.

Quadra-Trac is a permanent four-wheel-drive system with no front hubs to manually lock and unlock. It was a popular option, especially among drivers who liked the convenience of not having to bother with engaging the system. However, any permanent four-wheel-drive system does have a negative effect on mileage, and in 1980, Quadra-Trac was dropped and the Selec-Trac four-

wheel drive was made optional. It is a better system than the Quadra-Trac because it allows the use of a two-wheel drive for normal use, and by engaging a dash-mounted switch, the system goes into a full-time four-wheel-drive mode. Selec-Trac was only available with the automatic transmission.

A point worth remembering here is that manual drum brakes (until 1978) and manual steering were standard equipment for the most part on the Cherokee. Power front disc brakes and variable-ratio power steering are recommended options.

Like other Jeep vehicles made in the 1970s and early 1980s, the Cherokee is prone to rust. For that reason, try to find one built during 1981-83. A loaded Laredo or Chief can provide all the comforts anyone could want for winter and bad weather use.

Although the Cherokee is not considered a collectible yet, I believe that a properly optioned Chief will eventually start appre-

1977 also brought the Cherokee Chief. Wide wheel flares, large wheels and tires helped to give some pizzaz to the traditional looking Wagoneer body. AMC

ciating in value, however modestly, because of its good looks, relative technological advancement and its size. They'll never be built that big again. The Cherokee represents a time when big was still better.

**1974-83 Cherokee**
**BASE ENGINE**
Type . . . . . . . . . . . . . . . . . . . . . . . . . . . . inline 6-cyl ohv
Bore x stroke, in . . . . . . . . . . . . . . . . . . . . . 3.750x3.895
Displacement, cubic in . . . . . . . . . . . . . . . . . . . . 258
Compression ratio . . . . . . . . . . . . . . . . . . . . . . . 8.0:1
Horsepower . . . . . . . . . . . . . . . . . . . . . . . . . 110@3500
Torque . . . . . . . . . . . . . . . . . . . . . . . . . . . 195@2000
Optional engines . . . . . . . . 360 2-bbl V-8, 360 4-bbl V-8, 401 4-bbl V-8
**CHASSIS & DRIVETRAIN**
Clutch . . . . . . . . . . . . . . . . . . . . . . . . . single dry-plate
Transmission . . . . . . . . . 3-speed manual (4-speed opt, 3-speed auto opt)
Transfer case . . . . . . . . . . . . . . . . . . . . . . . . 2-speed
Front suspension . . . . . . . . . . . . . . . . . . . leaf springs
Rear suspension . . . . . . . . . . . . . . . . . . . leaf springs
Axle ratio . . . . . . . . . . . . . . . . . . . . . . . . . . various
Brakes, front/rear . . . . . . . . . . drum/drum, disc/drum opt
**GENERAL**
Wheelbase, in . . . . . . . . . . . . . . . . . . . . . . . . 109
Height, in . . . . . . . . . . . . . . . . . . . . . . . . . . 65.3
Width, in . . . . . . . . . . . . . . . . . . . . . . . . . . . 75.6
Length, in . . . . . . . . . . . . . . . . . . . . . . . . . . 183.7
Weight, lb . . . . . . . . . . . . . . . . . . . . . . . . . . 4,025
*Note: These specifications are for a 1975 Cherokee*

This 1979 Chief looks positively mean. AMC

1982 Cherokee Laredo—the ultimate in luxury.

The Cherokee's size, weight and excellent bad-weather performance make it an excellent emergency vehicle.

# Chapter 11

# Wrangler

The national press stirred a lot of patriotic feelings when it let it be known that AMC was planning to retire the venerable CJ. After all, the Jeep CJ-7 was the descendant of the jeep that helped win World War II, and it was as American as apple pie. There were even petitions made to AMC to keep the CJ in production. However, when the Wrangler

1986 Wrangler (known as the YJ in Canada). The Laredo version has chrome bumpers and grille. AMC

Wrangler is available with either a hard top or soft top. Soft top shown here is designed to be used with factory steel doors.

was finally introduced in early 1986, all the brouhaha died down.

The Wrangler, the CJ's replacement, isn't that much different. It is slightly smaller, and the rectangular headlights give it a more modern look, but AMC wisely did not change the basic Jeep shape. It is, though, a vast improvement over the CJ, especially in terms of ride and cornering ability. While the CJ's ride is stiff and very bumpy, the new Wrangler is a lot more pleasant to drive, but without losing its off-road capability.

Still, in spite of all the improvements, the Wrangler is no replacement for a regular passenger car. AMC, however, did quite a bit of research designing the Wrangler. For example, in 1978 AMC found that thirty-five percent of CJ owners used their Jeeps off-road, seventeen percent used them as personal transportation and only seven per-cent never went off-road. However, by 1984 the situation had changed dramatically. Seven percent went off-road, twenty percent never went off-road and ninety-five percent used them for personal transportation. People's tastes had changed, and although they did not go off-road as often as they had before, they still wanted the image of an off-road machine. At the same time, CJ sales had been declining and thus the Wrangler was designed with all this in mind.

The Wrangler borrows most of its mechanical components from the XJ (down-sized Cherokee) line: steering, brakes, front and rear axles, transfer case, five-speed transmission, hydraulic clutch, wheels, tires and engines. The Wrangler also utilizes the CJ's familiar body-on-frame construction. A standard 2.5 liter four-cylinder puts out 121 hp at 5250 rpm with 141 lb-ft torque at 3250

Redesigned dash provides more information and creates an up-to-date atmosphere.

rpm. The optional 4.2 liter six puts out less horsepower, 112 at 3000 rpm, but torque increases to 210 lb-ft at 2000 rpm. Currently, the four-cylinder five-speed is made by Aisin in Japan; the five-speed used on the six comes from Peugeot; and the three-speed automatic from Chrysler. Only the Command-Trac part-time four-wheel drive is available on the Wrangler.

Like its predecessor, the Wrangler is offered with two tops, a soft top and a hardtop—both transmitting outside wind noise. But in terms of sealing, they are a big improvement over the CJ's tops, which are notorious water leakers.

Inside, the biggest change is the dash. It is modern! Besides the speedometer and tachometer, there are four additional gauges and a clock. The roll bar is still standard equipment, and the high-back bucket seats still offer no rake adjustment (up to 1987).

The Wrangler is a worthy successor to the CJ, which will probably continue in its present form well into the 1990s. We may see the installation of more Chrysler driveline components, but it is certain that Chrysler will not attempt to alter the Wrangler from its present configuration.

| Wrangler | |
|---|---|
| **BASE ENGINE** | |
| Type | inline 4-cyl |
| Bore x stroke, in | 3.876x3.188 |
| Displacement, cubic in | 150 |
| Compression ratio | 9.2:1 |
| Horsepower | 117@5000 |
| Torque | 135@3500 |
| Optional engines | 258 ci inline 6 |
| **CHASSIS & DRIVETRAIN** | |
| Clutch | single dry-plate |
| Transmission | 5-speed manual |
| Transfer case | 2-speed |
| Front suspension | leaf springs |
| Rear suspension | leaf springs |
| Axle ratio | 4.11:1 |
| Brakes, front/rear | disc/drum |
| **GENERAL** | |
| Wheelbase, in | 93.4 |
| Height, in | 68.9 |
| Width, in | 66 |
| Length, in | 152 |
| Weight, lb | 2,869 (4-cyl), 3,023 (6-cyl) |

Rear seat folds down. Carpeting is a useful and desirable option.

Roll bar is slightly different from the CJ roll bar. The two cross bars provide more support. AMC refers to the roll bar as a Sports Bar. Roll is a dirty word at Jeep.

No big news here. Optional six-cylinder (shown) is more desirable over the base four-cylinder. At best, the six-cylinder can be termed adequate, but the Wrangler would be transformed with the Cherokee fuel-injected six.

1988 Wrangler Sahara. AMC

# Chapter 12

# Comanche

| ★★ Comanche |
|---|

In 1986, Jeep introduced its newest truck, the Comanche. Although this market segment is fairly well saturated and highly competitive, the Comanche has proven to be successful primarily because of its modern design and, of course, the Jeep name. Borrowing heavily from the existing Cherokee line, the Comanche was offered with the usual array of options, trim packages and the like, that distinguish domestic trucks from imports.

One important fact that distinguished the Comanche from all others was its bed size of seven feet. This falls in between the typical full-size pickup's eight feet, and the usual six feet for small pickups. For this reason, Jeep advertised it as the first *true* mid-size pickup. A short-bed version with a six-foot bed became available in 1987.

In addition, the Comanche is available in two-wheel-drive or four-wheel-drive versions. In 1986, the standard engine was the

Resemblance to the downsized Cherokee is obvious. The Comanche was first offered as a 1986 model in two-wheel-drive and four-wheel-drive forms. AMC

2.5 liter four-cylinder pumping out 121 hp. The 2.8 liter Chevy V-6 was optional, which has distinguished itself by its lack of power and lackluster reliability.

If you are interested in a Comanche, the one to get is a 1987 with the Jeep 4.0 liter inline six (Power-Tech six). Although it is the familiar six that AMC has used for years, sequential multipoint electronic fuel injection boosts horsepower to 173, which adds up to quite a ride, with 0-60 in nine seconds as compared to over eighteen seconds with the Chevy V-6.

The standard transmission with the four-cylinder engine is a four-speed manual, with a five-speed optional in most configurations. As far as automatics go, a three-speed automatic was all you could get in 1986. The 1987 models with the Power-Tech six came with a new four-speed automatic, which makes the most of the six's power output. It features two shift schedules—a comfort and a power setting. For normal driving, the comfort setting is all that is required. If additional acceleration is required, the power setting allows the engine to rev higher before a shift is made.

Suspension and brakes are identical to those found on the Cherokee, as is the four-wheel-drive system. The part-time Command-Trac is available on 1986-87 models; the full-time Selec-Trac only on 1986s.

It is quite likely that additional versions of the Comanche will be introduced in the coming years, such as a short-bed extended cab. It is unlikely that Chrysler will decide to discontinue the Comanche because it has proven to be a decent seller. However, it *is* quite likely that we'll see the increasing use of Chrysler components, as Jeep becomes an integrated part of Chrysler Corporation.

---

**Comanche**
**BASE ENGINE**

| | |
|---|---|
| Type | inline 4-cyl ohv |
| Bore x stroke, in | 3.876x3.188 |
| Displacement, cubic in | 150 |
| Compression ratio | 9.2:1 |
| Horsepower | 117@5000 |
| Torque | 135@3000 |
| Optional engines | 4.0 liter inline 6 |

**CHASSIS & DRIVETRAIN**

| | |
|---|---|
| Clutch | single dry-plate |
| Transmission | 4-speed manual (5-speed opt, 4-speed auto opt) |
| Transfer case | 2-speed |
| Front suspension | coil springs |
| Rear suspension | leaf springs |
| Axle ratio | various |
| Brakes, front/rear | disc/drum |

**GENERAL**

| | |
|---|---|
| Wheelbase, in | 112.9 |
| Height, in | 64 |
| Width, in | 71.7 |
| Length, in | 179.3 |
| Weight, lb | 3,025 |

*Note: These specifications are for a 1987 four-wheel-drive short-box Comanche*

1987 short-bed version. This is a Comanche
Chief. AMC

# Chapter 13

# Cherokee, Wagoneer Ltd.

| ★★ | Cherokee, Wagoneer Ltd., 1984-87 |
|----|----------------------------------|

The year 1984 saw the introduction of the downsized Cherokee, the fruit of the hundreds of millions of dollars Renault had poured into AMC since it obtained forty-six percent interest in AMC in 1979. If AMC and the Jeep line were to remain viable in the US market, the new Cherokee had to be successful.

The new downsized Cherokee has been a runaway success in spite of the fact that the Cherokee is more expensive than its Ford or GM competitors. The Cherokee also pro-

The downsized Cherokee has been AMC's savior. This is a 1985 Cherokee Chief. AMC

vided AMC with a platform to build the Comanche pickups, and the CJ's replacement, the Wrangler, uses many of its components. It is also the reason Chrysler bought out AMC in 1987.

There is no doubt that the Cherokee is indeed a handsome vehicle. Although it is slightly more angular than the Ford Bronco II or GM's S-10, it has more of the aggressive, rugged good looks that are associated with the name Jeep. However, an important reason for the Cherokee's success is that it has been available in a four-door, making it a viable alternative to the traditional station wagon for many families.

Structurally, the Cherokee differs from previous Jeeps in that it is a unibody-type design, rather than body-on-frame. This is a less expensive way to build, and provides a better and quieter ride, but it is less durable

from the off-road point of view—although not a major consideration with the bulk of today's Cherokee buyers. The front suspension also utilizes coil springs unlike previous Jeeps. Rear suspension is strictly conventional leaf springs.

A 2.5 liter four-cylinder has been the standard engine, with the 2.8 liter Chevy V-6 optional until 1987, when it was replaced with the AMC 4.0 liter inline six. (*Avoid* the V-6—it lacks power for even normal acceleration. If you floor it, all you get is lots of thrashing and noise and very little forward movement.) The inline six features multiport electronic fuel injection which helps account for its high, 173 hp rating.

Two manual transmissions have been offered: a four-speed, standard with the four-cylinder, and a five-speed for the sixes. In terms of automatics, the Chevrolet V-6

Four-door versions, such as this 1987 Laredo, are extremely popular; still the only domestic to be offered with four doors.

Wagoneer Limited is based on the downsized Cherokee platform. It is differentiated by grille design, and the suspension is calibrated for a quieter, smoother ride. This is a 1987. AMC was available with just a three-speed, while the AMC six is available with a four-speed automatic overdrive which features electronic shift control, a lock-up torque converter and two shift patterns. The normal setting allows the transmission to perform like any other automatic, while in the power setting, the transmission upshifts at a higher rpm, thus producing better acceleration. Definitely state of the art!

Two four-wheel-drive systems are available. A part-time system, Command-Trac, has shift-on-the-fly capability, while the optional Selec-Trac, available with automatics, is a full-time system. About the only thing missing from the Cherokee is ABS (antiskid brake system), which would make it an incredible winter/bad weather vehicle.

A Renault-built four-cylinder turbo-diesel measuring 2.1 liters, first available in 1987, has had extremely limited appeal and it was not offered again in 1988. Two-wheel-drive versions of the Cherokee also became available in 1986, again with very limited success.

In late 1987, the Cherokee Limited was introduced—basically every option standard equipment plus a leather interior. Available only in three colors, AMC describes the Limited as an "upscale" four-wheel-drive vehicle. This is the 1988 version.

| 1984-up Cherokee | |
|---|---|
| **BASE ENGINE** | |
| Type | 4-cyl ohv |
| Bore x stroke, in | 3.876x3.188 |
| Displacement, cubic in | 150 |
| Compression ratio | 9.2:1 |
| Horsepower | 117@5000 |
| Torque | 135@3000 |
| Optional engines | 2.1 liter 4-cyl diesel, 4.0 liter inline 6 |
| **CHASSIS & DRIVETRAIN** | |
| Clutch | single dry-plate |
| Transmission | 4-speed manual |
| Transfer case | 2-speed |
| Front suspension | coil springs |
| Rear suspension | leaf springs |
| Axle ratio | various |
| Brakes, front/rear | disc/drum |
| **GENERAL** | |
| Wheelbase, in | 101.4 |
| Height, in | 63.3 |
| Width, in | 70.5 |
| Length, in | 165.3 |
| Weight, lb | 3,600 |
| *Note: These specifications are for a 1987 Cherokee* | |

The Wagoneer and Wagoneer Ltd. are simply loaded-to-the-hilt Cherokees with a redesigned grille and woodgrain-type side treatment on the Wagoneer Ltd. They do have a more carlike ride, though.

It almost seems as if the Cherokee is not *really* considered to be an off-road vehicle, with so much emphasis on luxury. It is comfortable, luxurious and fast, and it can go where no car would dare.

Functional, well-designed interior comes with front bucket seats only.

Not as roomy as the Grand Wagoneer, the Cherokee nevertheless is more in tune with today's needs. Rear seat folds down.

Definitely avoid any Cherokee powered by the Chevy 2.8 V-6. Not enough power, and dismal reliability.

Optional from 1987 is the familiar AMC inline
six. Very reliable and very powerful.

The inline's length made it necessary for a fire-
wall modification.

Base engine is the AMC-designed four-cylinder.
It will get you there, eventually.

# Value guide

| Year | Model | Restorable | Good | Excellent |
|------|-------|-----------|------|-----------|
| 1946-53 | CJ-2A/CJ-3A | $100-500 | $1000-2000 | $2000-10,000 |
| 1952-64 | CJ3B | 100-500 | 1000-2000 | 2000-7500 |
| 1955-83 | CJ-5 | 100-500 | 1000-2000 | 2000-5000 |
| 1955-76 | CJ-6 | 100-500 | 1000-2000 | 2000-4500 |
| 1976-86 | CJ-7/Scrambler | 1000-2500 | 2500-5000 | 5000-8000 |
| 1946 | Station Wagon/Delivery | 800-1500 | 2500-5000 | 5000-9500 |
| 1948-51 | Jeepster | 1500-2500 | 2500-7000 | 7000-15,000 |
| 1946-up | Jeep Truck | 200-500 | 1000-2500 | 2500-5000 |
| 1957-64 | FC Truck | 100-500 | 1000-2000 | 2000-7500 |
| 1967-71 | Jeepster | 100-500 | 1000-2000 | 2000-5000 |
| 1972-73 | Commando | 100-500 | 1000-1500 | 1500-4000 |
| 1941-45 | MB | 100-500 | 1000-2500 | 2500-10,000 |
| 1950-52 | M38 | 100-500 | 1000-2500 | 2500-10,000 |
| 1952-71 | M38A1 | 100-500 | 1000-2000 | 2000-8000 |

# Parts and service sources

These are some of the many parts and service sources available.

Acme Truck Parts
P.O. Box 5252
Carson, CA 90749
   Body parts and accessories for CJ

Safari Auto Supply
23 N. Madison Ave.
Spring Valley, NY 10977
   Jeep parts and tops

The Jeepsterman
572 Ramtown Rd.
Howell, NJ 07731
   Jeepster, Jeep parts, literature

Beachwood Canvas Works
P.O. Box 137 W.
Island Heights, NJ 08732
   Canvas tops

Andrew Magyar
3536 Highland St.
Allentown, PA 18104
   Parts and information on all Jeeps

Carl Walck
719 Lehigh St.
Bowmanstown, PA 18030
   Parts, service, literature

Buz Bowling
P.O. Box 2282
Charlotte, NC 28211
   Military surplus vehicles and parts

Paul I. Politis
Automotive Literature
Box 335 HC 75
McConnellsburg, PA 17233
   Automotive literature specialist

John A. Conde
1340 Fieldway Dr.
Bloomfield Hills, MI 48013
   AMC & Jeep literature and information

# Clubs

The Willys Club
719 Lehigh St.
Bowmanstown, PA 18030
   Dedicated to Willys-built vehicles, 1933-63;
publishes *Willys World* bimonthly

The Willys Overland Jeepster Club
Box 12042
El Paso, TX 79913
   Dedicated to the 1948-51 Jeepster convertible, publishes monthly newsletter

# Suggested reading

*Military Jeeps 1941-45*
by R. M. Clarke
   Reprinted articles and road tests

*The Jeep*
edited by Bart H. Vanderveen
   Pictorial history of the Military Jeeps

*Hail to the Jeep*
by A. Wade Wells
   Reprint of an early pictorial history of
the Jeep in WWII

*Jeep: Mechanical mule to people's plaything*
photography by Henry Rasmussen
   Collection of photographs focusing on
modified and off-road CJs

*Jeep Collection No. 1, 1942-45*
by R.M. Clarke
   Reprinted articles and road tests

*Off-Road Jeeps: Civilian and Military 1944-71*
by R. M. Clarke
   Reprinted articles and road tests

# Production figures

The production figures presented here were provided by The Willys Club. Unfortunately, figures beyond 1961 are not available. All figures are for model years.

Some of the abbreviations used are listed below:

463 Four-cylinder 63 hp Go-Devil
663 Six-cylinder 63 hp Lightning
473 Four-cylinder 73 hp Hurricane
475 Four-cylinder 75 hp Hurricane
6-226 Six-cylinder Super Hurricane
SW station wagon
SD sedan delivery
PU pickup
STK stake body
ST.CH. stripped chassis
C/WS cowl and windshield
FFC flat face cowl

AMB ambulance
DUAL dual rear wheels

**CJ-2A**

| | |
|---|---|
| 1945 | 1,824 |
| 1946 | 71,554 |
| 1947 | 65,078 |
| 1948 | 74,122 |
| 1949 | 2,182 |

**CJ-3A**

| | |
|---|---|
| 1949 | 27,749 |
| 1950 | 26,034 |
| 1951 | 44,158 |
| 1952 | 29,655* |
| 1953 | 10,617 |

*Includes 13 stripped chassis

## CJ-3B

| | 1953 | 1954 | 1955 | 1956 | 1957 | 1958 | 1959 | 1960 | 1961 |
|---|---|---|---|---|---|---|---|---|---|
| CJ-3B | 27,551 | 31,292 | 12,952 | 11,418 | 7,220 | 6,656 | 9,300 | 9,926 | 12,485 |
| ST.CH. | 2,267 | 3,105 | 1,667 | 49 | 1 | 2 | 7 | | 73 |
| Fire Truck | 65 | 12 | 7 | 11 | 7 | 7 | 4 | 1 | 65 |
| Total | 29,883 | 34,409 | 11,418 | 11,478 | 7,228 | 6,665 | 9,311 | 9,927 | 12,983 |

## CJ-5

| | 1955 | 1956 | 1957 | 1958 | 1959 | 1960 | 1961 |
|---|---|---|---|---|---|---|---|
| CJ-5 | 17,006 | 18,915 | 22,893 | 14,062 | 15,040 | 21,621 | 15,208 |
| Fire Eng. | 1 | 6 | | 4 | 2 | 6 | |
| ST.CH. | 10 | 12 | 46 | 68 | 37 | 152 | 61 |
| C/WS | | 6 | 6 | 3 | 5 | | |
| Diesel | | | | | | | 152 |
| Total | 17,017 | 18,939 | 22,945 | 14,137 | 15,084 | 21,799 | 15,421 |

## CJ-6

| | 1956 | 1957 | 1958 | 1959 | 1960 | 1961 |
|---|---|---|---|---|---|---|
| CJ-6 | 2,224 | 1,639 | 1,214 | 2,006 | 2,036 | 1,991 |
| ST.CH. | 2 | 2 | | | | |
| Fire Eng. | | | | | | 4 |
| Diesel | | | | | | 28 |
| Total | 2,226 | 1,641 | 1,214 | 2,006 | 2,036 | 2,023 |

## Station Wagon/Sedan Delivery

| | | |
|---|---|---|
| 1946 | 463 | 6,534 |
| 1947 | 463 | 27,515 |
| 1948 | 463 | 40,774 |
| | 663 | 3,607 |
| 1949 | 463 | 23,069 |
| | 663 | 10,006 |
| | 4x463 SW | 4,472 |
| | Total | 37,547 |
| 1950 | 463 | 4,506 |
| | 663 | 2,322 |
| | 473 SW | 19,616 |
| | 673 SW | 7,931 |
| | 4x463 SW | 3,086 |
| | 4x473 SW-SD | 2,450 |
| | Total | 39,911 |
| 1951 | 473 SW | 15,906 |
| | 673 SW | 8,470 |
| | 4x473 SW | 11,854 |
| | 2x473 SW | 630 |
| | SD | 135 |
| | Total | 36,995 |

| | | |
|---|---|---|
| 1952 | 475 SW | 4,277 |
| | 473 SD | 2,091 |
| | 2x475 SW | 18 |
| | 4x475 SW-SD | 5,683 |
| | Total | 12,069 |
| 1953 | 475 SW | 4,747 |
| | 475 SD | 2,347 |
| | 2x475 SD | 94 |
| | 4x475 SW | 10,631 |
| | SD | 992 |
| | Total | 18,811 |
| 1954 | 475 SW | 188 |
| | SD | 148 |
| | 6-226 4x4 SW | 2,645 |
| | SD | 219 |
| | 4x475 SW | 3,528 |
| | SD | 288 |
| | SD* | 100 |
| | Total | 7,116 |
| | *Post Office | |

| 1955 | 475 | SW | 98 |
| | | SD | 98 |
| | 475 2x4 | SW | 70 |
| | | SD | 84 |
| | | 4x4 SW | 1,275 |
| | | SD | 174 |
| | | C/WS | 6 |
| | 6-226 2x4 | SW | 845 |
| | | SD | 226 |
| | | ST.CH. | 1 |
| | | AMB | 2 |
| | | 4x4 SW | 13,095 |
| | | SD | 5,890 |
| | | ST.CH. | 2 |
| | | FFC | 3 |
| | | C/WS | 1 |
| | | AMB | 5 |
| | **Total** | | 21,875 |
| | | | |
| 1956 | 475 2x4 | SW | 2,510 |
| | | SD | 324 |
| | | ST.CH. | 491 |
| | | 4x4 SW | 1,664 |
| | | SD | 222 |
| | | FFC | 1 |
| | | AMB | 28 |
| | 6-226 2x4 | SW | 1,344 |
| | | SD | 374 |
| | | AMB | 2 |
| | | 4x4 SW | 7,239 |
| | | SD | 759 |
| | | AMB | 11 |
| | | RT | 2 |
| | **Total** | | 14,970 |
| | | | |
| 1957 | 475 2x4 | SW | 535 |
| | | SD | 430 |
| | | AMB | 9 |
| | | 4x4 SW | 1,310 |
| | | SD | 282 |
| | | FFC | 3 |
| | | AMB | 32 |
| | 6-226 2x4 | SW | 2,477 |
| | | SD | 238 |
| | | AMB | 4 |
| | | 4x4 SW | 7,364 |
| | | SD | 780 |
| | | FFC | 1 |
| | | AMB | 21 |
| | | RT | 7 |
| | **Total** | | 13,493 |

| 1958 | 475 2x4 | SW | 69 |
| | | SD | 418 |
| | | ST.CH. | 60 |
| | | AMB | 1 |
| | | Maverick | 100 |
| | | 4x4 SW | 493 |
| | | SD | 259 |
| | | AMB | 8 |
| | 6-226 2x4 | SW | 585 |
| | | SD | 200 |
| | | AMB | 4 |
| | | 4x4 SW | 6,497 |
| | | SD | 536 |
| | | AMB | 16 |
| | | RT | 2 |
| | **Total** | | 9,248 |
| | | | |
| 1959 | 475 2x4 | SW | 241 |
| | | SD | 436 |
| | | ST.CH. | 103 |
| | | AMB | 2 |
| | | Maverick | 2,553 |
| | | 4x4 SW | 1,352 |
| | | SD | 140 |
| | 6-226 2x4 | SW | 350 |
| | | SD | 238 |
| | | AMB | 32 |
| | | Maverick | 130 |
| | | 4x4 SW | 8,165 |
| | | SD | 550 |
| | | FFC | 1 |
| | | AMB | 45 |
| | | RT | 2 |
| | **Total** | | 14,340 |
| | | | |
| 1960 | 475 2x4 | SW | 56 |
| | | SD | 484 |
| | | ST.CH. | 90 |
| | | SW* | 2,566 |
| | | 4x4 SW | 1,175 |
| | | SD | 127 |
| | | AMB | 93 |
| | 6-226 2x4 | SW | 80 |
| | | SD | 418 |
| | | SW* | 968 |
| | | 4x4 SW | 8,968 |
| | | SD | 1,246 |
| | | AMB | 169 |
| | **Total** | | 16,440 |

*Facelift*

| | | | |
|---|---|---|---|
| 1961 | 475 2x4 SW | 213 | |
| | Maverick | 202 | |
| | 4x4 SW | 840 | |
| | SD | 556 | |
| | AMB | 55 | |
| | 6-226 2x4 SD | 251 | |
| | AMB | 75 | |
| | AY | 376 | |
| | 4x4 SW | 7,908 | |
| | SD | 749 | |
| | ST.CH. | 1 | |
| | C/WS | 90 | |
| | CAB | 123 | |
| | Total | 11,429 | |

## Jeep Truck

| | | |
|---|---|---|
| 1947 | 2WD (2T) | 2,642 |
| | 4WD (4T) | 2,346 |
| | Total | 4,988 |
| 1948 | 2WD (2T) | 9,216 |
| | 4WD (4T) | 20,957 |
| | Total | 30,173 |
| 1949 | 2WD (2T) | 4,955 |
| | 4WD (4T) | 19,757 |
| | Total | 15,712 |
| 1950 | 2WD (2T) | 971 |
| | 4WD (4T) | 3,646 |
| | 473 HT | 4,679 |
| | 4WD | 9,338 |
| | Total | 18,634 |
| 1951 | 473 HT PU | |
| | CAB | 1,070 |
| | STK | |
| | 4WD PU | 16,029 |
| | CAB | 1,894 |
| | STK | 420 |
| | Total | 38,047 |
| 1952 | 473 4WD PU | 13,183 |
| | STK | 358 |
| | C/WS | 56 |
| | CAB | 1,085 |
| | FFC | 1,473 |
| | Total | 16,155 |

| | | |
|---|---|---|
| 1953 | 475 4WD PU | 14,128 |
| | STK | 694 |
| | CAB | 1,522 |
| | C/WS | 8 |
| | FFC | 146 |
| | Total | 16,498 |
| 1954 | 475 4WD PU | 3,594 |
| | STK | 185 |
| | CAB | 681 |
| | FFC | 13 |
| | C/WS | 4 |
| | Total | 4,477 |
| 1955 | 475 4WD PU | 922 |
| | STK | 26 |
| | CAB | 558 |
| | C/WS | 7 |
| | 6-226 4WD PU | 168 |
| | STK | 5,691 |
| | CAB | 6,391 |
| | C/WS | 50 |
| | ST.CH. | 1 |
| | Fire Truck | 1 |
| | AMB | 11 |
| | CPC | 30 |
| | Total | 13,856 |
| 1956 | 475 4WD PU | 609 |
| | STK | 33 |
| | CAB | 372 |
| | C/WS | 606 |
| | FFC | 2 |
| | AMB | 10 |
| | CPC | 62 |
| | 6-226 4WD PU | 11,277 |
| | STK | 568 |
| | CAB | 3,066 |
| | C/WS | 15 |
| | ST.CH. | 1 |
| | AMB | 29 |
| | 475 2WD PU | 4 |
| | Total | 16,654 |

| 1957 | **475 4WD PU** | 731 |
| | STK | 31 |
| | CAB | 156 |
| | C/WS | 505 |
| | FFC | 1 |
| | AMB | 28 |
| | CPC | 15 |
| | **6-226 4WD PU** | 6,708 |
| | STK | 388 |
| | CAB | 1,018 |
| | C/WS | 13 |
| | **Total** | 9,594 |

| 1958 | **475 4WD PU** | 488 |
| | STK | 7 |
| | CAB | 185 |
| | C/WS | 108 |
| | FFC | 2 |
| | AMB | 11 |
| | CPC | 14 |
| | **6-226 4WD PU** | 5,660 |
| | STK | 348 |
| | CAB | 1,493 |
| | C/WS | 6 |
| | FFC | 22 |
| | Fire Eng. | 21 |
| | AMB | 40 |
| | CPC | 39 |
| | AVA | 1 |
| | **Total** | 8,445 |

| 1959 | **475 4WD PU** | 233 |
| | STK | 4 |
| | CAB | 206 |
| | C/WS | 659 |
| | FEC | 1 |
| | AMB | 2 |
| | CPC | 10 |
| | **6-226 4WD PU** | 7,412 |
| | STK | 510 |
| | CAB | 2,608 |
| | C/WS | 6 |
| | FFC | 23 |
| | AMB | 6 |
| | CPC | 60 |
| | Fire Eng. | 2 |
| | **Total** | 11,742 |

| 1960 | **475 4WD PU** | 531 |
| | STK | 100 |
| | CAB | 124 |
| | C/WS | 1,451 |
| | AMB | 4 |
| | **6-226 4WD PU** | 7,627 |
| | STK | 604 |
| | CAB | 3,622 |
| | C/WS | 12 |
| | FFC | 83 |
| | AMB | 111 |
| | CPC | 135 |
| | **2x4 C/WS** | 73 |
| | **475 2x4 FFC** | 202 |
| | **Total** | 14,636 |

| 1961 | **475 4WD PU** | 316 |
| | STK | 4 |
| | CAB | 59 |
| | C/WS | 23 |
| | CPC | 351 |
| | **6-226 4WD PU** | 255 |
| | STK | 412 |
| | CAB | 1,911 |
| | C/WS | 11 |
| | ST.CH. | 104 |
| | FFC | 55 |
| | AMB | 10 |
| | CPC | 35 |
| | **Total** | 3,546 |

**Jeepster**

| 1948 | **463 VJ2** | 10,326 |
| 1949 | **463 VJ2** | 2,307 |
| | **663 VJ3** | 654 |
| | **Total** | 2,961 |
| 1950 | **473 VJ3** | 4,066 |
| | **673 VJ3** | 1,779 |
| | **Total** | 5,845 |

**FC150/FC170**

| 1957 | **FC150 CAB** | 6,635 |
| | ST.CH. | 2 |
| | **FC170 CAB** | 3,101 |
| | **Total** | 9,738 |

**141**

| 1958 | FC150 CAB | 2,070 |
| | C/WS | 1 |
| | ST.CH. | 1 |
| | **Total** | 2,072 |
| | FC170 CAB | 1,519 |
| | C/WS | 3 |
| | **Total** | 1,522 |
| 1960 | FC150 CAB | 1,924 |
| | ST.CH. | 1 |
| | **Total** | 1,925 |
| | FC170 CAB | 2,506 |
| | ST.CH. | 96 |
| | DUAL | 402 |
| | **Total** | 3,004 |
| 1961 | FC150 CAB | 1,298 |
| | FC170 CAB | 2,047 |
| | ST.CH. | 6 |
| | DUAL | 320 |
| | **Total** | 3,671 |

**Calendar year production**

| 1970 | 45,805 |
| 1971 | 53,051 |
| 1972 | 71,204 |
| 1973 | 94,035 |
| 1974 | 96,645 |
| 1975 | 105,933 |
| 1976 | 126,742 |
| 1977 | 155,960 |
| 1978 | 180,514 |
| 1979 | 187,709 |
| 1980 | 92,094 |
| 1981 | 92,248 |
| 1982 | 85,742 |
| 1983 | 113,230 |
| 1984 | 187,086 |
| 1985 | 236,453 |
| 1986 | 220,896 |

The following production figures were provided by American Motors.

## CJ production

| Year | CJ2A | CJ3A | CJ3B | MC | MD | MDA | CJ5 | CJ6 | DJ3A | CJ5A | CJ6A | DJ5A | DJ6A | C101 | CJ7 | CJ8 |
|---|---|---|---|---|---|---|---|---|---|---|---|---|---|---|---|---|
| 1945 | 1824 | | | | | | | | | | | | | | | |
| 1946 | 71455 | | | | | | | | | | | | | | | |
| 1947 | 77958 | | | | | | | | | | | | | | | |
| 1948 | 62861 | 309 | | | | | | | | | | | | | | |
| 1949 | 104 | 31491 | | | | | | | | | | | | | | |
| 1950 | | 24060 | | 1563 | | | | | | | | | | | | |
| 1951 | | 40121 | | 13317 | | | | | | | | | | | | |
| 1952 | | 34654 | 2360 | 22972 | 29769 | | | | | | | | | | | |
| 1953 | | 1208 | 33047 | 23571 | 29769 | 2 | | | | | | | | | | |
| 1954 | | | 35972 | | 9560 | 1722 | 3883 | | | | | | | | | |
| 1955 | | | 12567 | | 8826 | 2271 | 23595 | 581 | 1316 | | | | | | | |
| 1956 | | | 10145 | | 3166 | | 18441 | 2523 | 1491 | | | | | | | |
| 1957 | | | 5756 | | 1050 | | 20819 | 1236 | 1248 | | | | | | | |
| 1958 | | | 6178 | | 780 | | 12401 | 1387 | 1175 | | | | | | | |
| 1959 | | | 5420 | | 1273 | | 17488 | 1947 | 2509 | | | | | | | |
| 1960 | | | 6139 | | 2673 | | 19753 | 2201 | 2360 | | | | | | | |
| 1961 | | | 1147 | | 434 | | 2064 | 244 | 199 | | | | | | | |
| 1962 | | | 9416 | | 2957 | 1155 | 14072 | 2502 | 1326 | | | | | | | |
| 1963 | | | 9801 | | 4369 | 464 | 12499 | 1534 | 1123 | | | | | | | |
| 1964 | | | 5271 | | 2622 | | 16029 | 1702 | 809 | 4128 | 164 | 1 | | | | |
| 1965 | | | 2847 | | 578 | 43 | 21014 | 2062 | 50 | 1987 | 115 | 1316 | 168 | | | |
| 1966 | | | 5459 | | 320 | 77 | 17974 | 3521 | | 1190 | 160 | 443 | 720 | 2345 | | |
| 1967 | | | 2523 | | 840 | 147 | 18186 | 2295 | | 89 | 20 | 1042 | 791 | 12621 | | |
| 1968 | | | 1446 | | 1906 | | 19683 | 2395 | | | | 521 | 627 | 13924 | | |
| 1969 | | | | | | | 20262 | 2433 | | | | 386 | 467 | 11289 | | |
| 1970 | | | | | | | 13518 | 2234 | | | | 254 | 467 | 9268 | | |
| 1971 | | | | | 596 | | 12559 | 1806 | | | | 153 | 949 | 7903 | | |
| 1972 | | | | | | | 22601 | 1175 | | | | 87 | 141 | 10685 | | |
| 1973 | | | | | | | 30449 | 1720 | | | | 102 | 23 | 9538 | | |
| 1974 | | | | | | | 43087 | 2826 | | | | | | | | |
| 1975 | | | | | | | 32486 | 2935 | | | | | | | | |
| 1976 | | | | | | | 31116 | 2431 | | | | | | | 21016 | |
| 1977 | | | | | | | 32996 | 2754 | | | | | | | 25414 | |
| 1978 | | | | | | | 37611 | 743 | | | | | | | 38274 | |
| 1979 | | | | | | | 41501 | 992 | | | | | | | 55264 | |
| 1980 | | | | | | | 24574 | 1633 | | | | | | | 38183 | |
| 1981 | | | | | | | 13477 | 360 | | | | | | | 27767 | 8355 |
| 1982 | | | | | | | 6080 | | | | | | | | 23820 | 7759 |
| 1983 | | | | | | | 3085 | | | | | | | | 37673 | 5405 |
| 1984 | | | | | | | | | | | | | | | 42644 | 4130 |
| 1985 | | | | | | | | | | | | | | | 43315 | 2015 |
| 1986 | | | | | | | | | | | | | | | 25929 | 128 |
| **Total** | 214202 | 131843 | 155494 | 61423 | 101488 | 5881 | 603303 | 50172 | 13606 | 7394 | 459 | 4305 | 4353 | 77573 | 379299 | 27792 |

Notes:
CJ5 & CJ7 Brampton Production 1979 thru 1980 — total 81640 included in the above
MC, MD and MDA are the Military Jeeps
C101 is known as the Jeepster Commando
CJ8 is known as the Scrambler